The Magic Bird

Folk Tales from China

(Seventh Series)

FOREIGN LANGUAGES PRESS   BEIJING

First Edition   1985

Edited by Ellen Hertz

ISBN   0-8351-1315-9

Published by the Foreign Languages Press
24 Baiwanzhuang Road, Beijing, China

Printed by the Foreign Languages Printing House
19 West Chegongzhuang Road, Beijing, China

Distributed by China International Book Trading Corporation
(Guoji Shudian), P.O. Box 399, Beijing, China

Printed in the People's Republic of China

Contents

Li Bao and Cui Cui

(*Han Nationality*)

Once upon a time there lived a little boy named Li Bao. When Li Bao was very young his mother died and his father remarried. His step-mother was a wicked woman who had her greedy eyes fixed on the family property. As the days passed and Li Bao grew older, she devised a plan to get rid of him so that her own son could inherit all for himself.

One day the vicious step-mother, pretending to be deeply concerned for Li Bao, said to him:

"Little Bao! You're almost a grown man, and you'll need to get yourself a wife soon. But our family is so poor, who would be willing to marry into this life of toil and hardship? We have to think of a way to save up some money to get you a bride!" And, before Li Bao could catch his breath she added:

"Today, I will give you two head of cattle, a cow and a bull. Go to the mountains and take good care of them, and when you have one hundred calves, you may return home. We can use the money from the calves to get you a

1

wife. . . . If you're a man at all, don't come back with even one less than one hundred calves. Don't expect me to bring up a son who does not keep his promises!"

These words hurt Li Bao deeply, and he burst into tears. He thought to himself, "how long will it take for two cows to produce one hundred calves! The mountains are full of wild beasts, and there's no telling — maybe they'll eat my cattle and me up in one bite!" The more he thought, the more apparent it became to him that his step-mother meant to kill him! "Even if I am eaten by wolves," he wondered, "it's still better than living in the same house with my step-mother." And so, he gritted his teeth and set off for the mountains.

Driving the cattle with his whip in one hand, the other hand steadying his shoulder pole hung with his pot and spoon and an old quilt, he walked until he came to the mountains. Over hill and dale he wandered, finally coming upon a hillside covered with green grass and exposed to the sun. A clear stream trickled out from a crack in the stone, and beside the stream flourished a grove of pine and cypress trees. Nestled within this grove, Li Bao found a mountain shrine built out of rock from the hillside, intact but completely deserted. Li Bao picked some wild grasses, tied them into a broom, and swept the place clean. Then he collected some more grass and leaves and arranged them into a pallet against the wall. He found three large stones and piled them up to form an oven. On the west wall stood a cowshed which would protect his cattle from wild animals at night. With this comfortable new home, Li Bao settled down happily to pass his life.

One day after breakfast Li Bao took up his whip and led the cattle out to the slope to graze. He lay down on his

side to watch them, but it did not take long for the soft "crunch, crunch" of their chewing to put him fast asleep. When he woke up it was almost noon. He stretched lazily, and was just picking up his whip to drive the cattle home for lunch when he saw two snakes, one green and one white, fighting as if for their lives down the hillside. They were locked in struggle, each with its teeth in the other's neck, and it seemed neither would escape with its life. In one stride, Li Bao rushed over to where the snakes were fighting and gave a sharp crack of his whip just in between the struggling snakes. The stunned beasts loosened their grip on each others' necks and slithered away, the green snake towards the southwest, the white snake towards the northeast, and in an instant they had vanished from sight.

The next day Li Bao ate his breakfast as usual, and then took the cattle out to pasture. Just as he had found himself a comfortable rock to sit on and was settling down for his morning nap, he heard a voice calling his name:

"Li Bao! Li Bao!"

He lifted his head, but saw no one. Who would venture into these mountains only to be eaten by wolves, he thought to himself. My ears must be playing tricks on me. He listened for a moment, and sure enough, the voice came again. Li Bao stood up and said loudly:

"Whoever you are, come out, please! Don't play tricks on a poor man like me." No sooner had these words left his mouth than there was a tap on his shoulder and a voice behind him said: "Over here."

Li Bao turned to find a young man dressed all in green wearing a green hat and smiling at him. Li Bao stood stunned. He had never in his stay in these deserted mountains seen a single person. Now here was someone he could talk to! He couldn't believe his good fortune.

"Li Bao, don't you recognize me? My name is Little Green. Yesterday I got into a fight with Little White right over there. If you hadn't saved me, I would have had my head bitten off. When I got home yesterday I told my father and mother about you, and they want you to come to our house for a visit. Will you follow me?"

But Li Bao declined. "If I go, there will be no one to look after my cattle and I'm afraid they will run away, or get eaten by wolves or tigers."

But Little Green answered in all seriousness, "If your cattle aren't here when you get back, I promise to pay you back with one hundred donkeys."

So, Li Bao tied his cattle securely and followed Little Green to the southwest, finally arriving at the entrance to a mountain cave. Little Green stopped, and pointed to the cave, saying:

"Li Bao. This is our home. Tonight after dinner my father is going to offer you a gift. Let me give you my advice. Up here in the mountains, gold and silver are useless. Ask for the date-wood stick that hangs behind the door. It is a magic stick, our family treasure, and has been handed down from generation to generation. If you meet wild beasts or bandits, all you have to do is to throw the stick up into the air and say: 'Magic stick! Magic stick! Show your power and protect Li Bao!' and it will beat your enemies to death."

Li Bao followed Little Green into the cave, which became wider and wider, and lighter and lighter, until finally they came upon a great walled compound of even green brick. To the left and right of the huge stone archway which was the front gate sat two stone lions. As they approached, the great black front door opened wide with a groan and out came an old man with a long white beard and an old woman with snow-white hair, who smiled broadly and said:

"Li Bao! Welcome! How can we thank you for saving our child's life?" And they gestured Li Bao to go ahead into their reception room.

Water was brought for Li Bao to wash his face, and tea was brought for his thirst, and then they all sat down to table. Out came one steaming-hot dish after another, each more delicious than the last. Li Bao had never in his life seen such a sumptuous repast, and he ate and drank until he could eat and drink no more. After the feast was over just as Li Bao was about to say goodbye the old host called a servant to bring out a platter full of silver and a platter full of gold. The old man said to Li Bao:

"You have saved our son's life, and though we have nothing much to offer you, please accept these tokens of our respect and thanks."

"As for saving people when they are in difficulty, it

is my duty." Li Bao began. "I have already been so magnificently entertained, so how can I accept these gifts as well?"

"That will never do! You had the compassion to save my son, so may I not repay part of this kindness?"

And so they argued back and forth, until finally the old man had no choice but to say:

"I have a proposal. You may take from our house anything you particularly like. In this way, perhaps you will accept our expression of thanks!"

Li Bao looked all around the room, and finally caught sight of the date-wood stick hanging behind the door. He brightened up, and said a little embarrassedly:

". . . I would like that date-wood stick! If I run into wild animals in the mountains, it will help me protect myself."

The old man hesitated for a moment and then said: "Very well! You may take it. But use it carefully. You may use it to protect yourself, but you mustn't use it to hurt others. Little Green, see our guest to the door!"

Little Green saw Li Bao as far as the little path out of the cave, hesitating a moment before saying: "Brother Li Bao, I will be frank with you. Yesterday, I fought with Little White because I wanted the fragrant lily which is their family treasure. He would not give it to me and instead called me an evil spirit. That is why we began to fight. I am sure that Little White will invite you to his house to thank you for saving his life. When his family offers you gifts, don't accept anything but that lily. This lily. . . . Well, you will know soon enough. For heaven's sake, don't forget. Goodbye." And, in the blink of an eye, Little Green turned into a little green snake and slithered away to the south.

The next day after breakfast, just as Little Bao was getting ready to let the cattle out of their shed, he saw far in the distance a young man dressed all in white with a white hat, striding towards him and waving his hand. "Li Bao! Li Bao!" he called. Li Bao thought to himself, this must be Little White. Little Green told me about him, and he called back:

"Who are you? How do you know my name?"

"My name is Little White. The day before yesterday you saved my life, don't you remember? I came looking for you yesterday to invite you to my house, but I found nothing but your cattle grazing in the pasture. Today I have returned. Will you come with me, please?"

"I cannot. If my cattle get eaten by tigers, my mother will beat me."

"Never fear," said Little White. "If you're missing a hair off either of your cattle, I promise to pay you back with a hundred horses."

So, once again Li Bao set off, this time towards the northeast. They walked for a long time, over hill and dale, and finally reached the entrance to a cave. Little White stopped and said: "This is my home."

The two had not gone too far into the cave when there opened out before them an expanse of level ground covered with mysterious flowers and magical herbs. Rare birds flew in the sky above them, and strange beasts crawled on the ground. Following a path paved with coloured stones, they walked as far as a small pavilion surrounded by a lotus pond. Emerald green gauze covered the beautiful latticework of the windows. They pushed past the pearl curtains hanging before the door and entered the pavilion. Little White poured some cool tea into a crystal glass for Li Bao to drink, and then said:

"Brother Li Bao! Please excuse me for a moment while I go to fetch my father and mother." While Little White was away, Li Bao took a good look around: the floor was inlaid with coloured stones in the patterns of birds; the chairs and benches were made from deep rose-coloured sandalwood; the teapot which sat on the table was remarkably delicate. . . . All the colours and shapes were so natural and alluring.

The sound of footsteps came from outside the door, and the pearl curtain was pushed aside. A stooped, old man, with a long white beard entered the room with his silver-haired wife. They smiled to Li Bao as they said warmly:

"Little White tried twice to invite you. We're so glad he finally succeeded. Please sit down. If it hadn't been for you showing mercy and saving Little White's life, he would have been dead for two days by now. Little White, have the wine and dishes brought in."

In came two maids, who soon had the table ready for

a feast.   No sooner had they finished than the most delicious food appeared before the delighted Li Bao.

After they had eaten and drunk their fill, Li Bao announced that he had to return to look after his cattle.   But
before he could go, Little White called to the servants
who brought in tray after tray of gleaming gold and pure
white pearls and presented them to Li Bao.

Remembering Little Green's advice, Li Bao refused all
of his gold and pearls outright. Instead, he pointed with
embarrassment to the fragrant lily and said:

"This flower seems to be healthy and it is very lovely.
Could you give me it instead?"

A look of unhappiness flashed across the old man's
face, and tears as big as beans slipped down his wife's
cheeks.   Little White looked at his parents and did not
say a word.   Li Bao hurriedly said:

"Oh, please don't be sad. I don't want the flower.
I will leave now." He made to go. But Little White
stopped him and then went over to his father and mother.
He whispered with them for a moment, the old couple
nodding their heads the whole time, and when they looked
up their expressions were cheerful:

"Li Bao! Please do not be angry with us.   There is a
reason for this, but we cannot tell you just yet.   After a
few days, you will find out for yourself.   Since you like
this flower, go ahead and take it.   But, please take very
good care of it!"   Having said this, the parents turned to
Little White and said:

"Take the flower and see Li Bao out, would you?" Then they begged Li Bao again: "Whatever you do, do not let this flower get blown by the wind, or pelted by the rain. Do not let it suffer any hardship, please remember!"

Little White carried the flower and led Li Bao out of the cave. Li Bao urged him again and again to turn back, but it was as if Little White could not bear to be separated from Li Bao. He accompanied him the entire way home, all the way to where he had fought with Little Green.

Then, Little White calmly handed the flower over to Li Bao and said: "I hope you will do as my parents have asked. Do not mistreat it. . . ." Then, he pulled out his handkerchief, wiped the tears from his eyes, said a final goodbye and ran off towards the northeast.

Li Bao felt utterly confused. How could this one flower be the cause of such a fight between Little Green and Little White? Why were the old man and woman so willing to give him gold and pearls, and so reluctant to give him this one flower? The more he thought, the less he could understand it. The scenes of the past two days filled his head, and he had no idea how to go about figuring them out.

He walked on carrying the flower, which became heavier with each step. Li Bao was soon exhausted and covered in sweat. Stopping to put down the flower for a moment, he was just going to wipe the sweat from his face when he looked up to notice that the end of the rope securing his cattle was untied. He hurried over and tugged on the end of the rope, and the cattle, seeing that he had returned, came and nuzzled him, licking his hand with their tongues. They seemed unusually affectionate, and thinking that it was late and perhaps the cattle were thirsty, he led them to the little stream to drink. Just at that moment, he heard a soft voice calling from behind:

"Brother Li Bao! Why have you abandoned me like this?" Li Bao turned his head to see a young maiden calling to him. She looked almost like a fairy, dressed all in emerald green silk. Li Bao was amazed and delighted, but even more confused. The beautiful maiden smiled at him and said:

"Brother Li Bao! Have you forgotten all that my parents and brother told you? One look at your cattle and you forget everything."

Li Bao could only ask stupidly: "Who are you?"

"My name is Cui Cui. I am Little White's older sister. You know the fragrant lily you were just carrying? That was me."

Without knowing it, they had walked to the front of the temple by this time, and Li Bao tied up his cattle and took Cui Cui into his home. He lowered his head and said with embarrassment: "Young maiden. I didn't know that you were that flower. Otherwise, a poor bachelor like myself would never dare allow a beautiful, cultivated girl like you to come here to this mountain hut to live in misery. While it is still light, let me take you back home."

Cui Cui laughed and said: "Li Bao, I'll tell you the truth. When I was young I often went to your village to play, and I know you are a kind person. Your step-mother tormented you in every way, but you were always diligent, brave and noble. Ever since you were sent to the mountains to herd cattle, I have come everyday to see you, though you didn't know it. And if one day I could not see you, I could neither eat nor sleep. I have been looking for a chance to talk to you, but I'm very shy." She stopped for a moment and then continued. "Little Green is the only son of my father's sister, and he has been spoiled from childhood. All he knows is how to stick out his arms to be dressed in the morning, and how to open his mouth when delicious food is brought to him. He has many bad ways. He has come to ask for my hand in marriage many times, but I never pay any attention to him. Now, he has started coming to our home to plead with my parents, but because he is their nephew, they feel they cannot tell him directly to go away. Finally, they asked Little White to tell him that I was not willing, and to make him give up the whole idea. But, Little Green was furious when he heard this and started a fight with Little White. Thankfully, you were there to break it up, and with Little White's help, you and I are together today. If you have any doubts about me, or you are not happy with me, I will not bother you, and I'll leave immediately."

"Don't be silly!" Li Bao hurriedly replied. "How could I suspect you?" He set about making dinner right away.

"The two of us were so wrapped up in talking we forgot that it was getting late," Cui Cui said. "Hurry and bring in the cattle."

Li Bao did as he was told, and when he returned he found a dish of fried pheasant and a dish of fresh fried mushrooms sitting on the stone table next to a platter of steaming rolls.

Li Bao asked in amazement: "Where did these come from?"

But Cui Cui only laughed, saying: "Don't ask where these dishes come from. Have a look over there!" Cui Cui pointed to the east wall of the room. Li Bao's pallet had vanished, and in its place stood a large double bed with a bright green quilt over a red blanket, and even embroidered pillows for two.

14

Li Bao said happily: "I see that with you I never need worry about anything."

And from that night on, they were the happiest of married couples.

The next day Cui Cui said: "Li Bao, look at the geese in the sky flying in pairs, and the ants on the ground working in their community. The two of us cannot live like this, all alone in the mountains. Let's go back to your home today!"

"That will never do! My father is dead, and my step-mother is head of the house now. When I lived with them I suffered every day. How could I ask you to return and suffer that way. Anyway, when I set out for the mountains my step-mother told me not be return until I had one hundred calves, not one less. How could I return now empty-handed?"

"Why, a hundred calves is nothing! Don't worry. When we arrive at your home I will handle everything."

Li Bao was not so sure, but he felt embarrassed to ask further. So, they packed up their things, and with Cui Cui riding the cow, and Li Bao in front driving the bull down the mountain slopes, they finally arrived at the village just as the sun was in the south.

Cui Cui took the whip from Li Bao's hand, and waved it in the air as she said:

"One lash to the east, one lash to the west. One hundred calves, appear!"

Before the words were out of her mouth, sure enough,

one hundred calves came running over. The calves' coats shone in the sunlight as they frolicked about, healthy and fat, lowing in delight. Li Bao led the old bull, and the one hundred young calves crowded behind. They entered the village just as the villagers were sitting down to lunch. Imagine their surprise at the sight of such strong, healthy calves and such a beautiful young maiden! Li Bao led the cattle into his courtyard, where they barely fit, they were so many.

His step-mother came out, and the first thing she did was count the calves. Indeed, there was neither one too many, nor one too few, but exactly one hundred. Now, this evil step-mother loved riches more than anything in the world, and seeing these one hundred calves her eyes lit up like lanterns as she said:

"Li Bao, you have brought me back all these calves, and in return I promise not to bring you any more trouble or suffering. Please, you and your wife live here at home with me."

And from that day on, Li Bao and Cui Cui lived and worked together happily ever after.

Translated by Ellen Hertz
Illustrated by Zhang Dayu

The Golden-haired Boy

(*Uygur Nationality*)

There was once a poor orphan called Xianiyazi. His
parents had long since passed away and although he was
still young, he had already started doing odd jobs for
others such as feeding animals, carrying water or sweeping the ground. In this way he was able to support himself
from day to day. One day, as he was lying asleep on his
brick bed, he dreamed that he saw a group of beautiful
young girls, bathing in a stream. They were splashing one
another and laughing merrily. Now one of these girls, called Nuerbaowa, was very lovely and kept smiling affec-
tionately at Xianiyazi. After splashing him with some
water, she ran off. Xianiyazi wanted to chase her, but
found that he was not quick enough. He began sweating
all over and then woke up with a start, to find that it had
all been no more than a beautiful dream. He was deeply
moved by this dream, and fell terribly in love with Nuerbaowa. But who knew where this girl lived, or how he
might find her? He thought about her day and night, his
heart becoming more and more restless. At last he decid-

ed to leave his village and search the world until he found
her.

Many months passed and after crossing countless rivers, mountains and deserts, Xianiyazi at last reached a

great city. He very much wanted to find work, but being a stranger there, he had no idea how to go about it. He wandered to the edge of the city and sat down forlornly next to a well. Just then, an old woman came along with a bucket to fetch water. Seeing the young man sitting there looking so dejected, she asked, "What is the matter, my child?"

Slowly raising his head, Xianiyazi replied, "I have my troubles, mother!"

"What are your troubles, my child? Have your parents driven you out?"

"No," replied Xianiyazi. "I have no parents. I am an orphan. I have come here to look for work, but being a stranger here I really do not know what to do. That is what I am worrying about."

"Stop all this nonsense!" said the old woman. "Why do you bring such troubles upon yourself? Come and live with me as my son. From now on I'll be as a mother to you. Come along, let's go home!"

Then picking up her bucket the old woman lead Xianiyazi back to her house. From that day on, Xianiyazi helped her, taking her cows out to graze and fetching water. One day, as he was driving the cows down the river to drink, he saw a group of girls bathing. One of these girls was extremely beautiful and it seemed to him that he had seen her somewhere before, but he could not recall where. So he hid himself near the riverbank and watched the girls splashing each other in the water.

Just then one of the girls called out, "Nuerbaowa!" and instantly Xianiyazi realized that this was none other than the girl of his dream whom he had searched for all this time. Overjoyed, he said to himself, "I have found her at last!"

Then quickly he picked a reed, from which he made a reed pipe. Sitting beneath a tree he began to play a melancholy tune. Hearing this melody the girls felt rather startled, but as they listened they gradually became more and more enchanted. At last they came out of the water, dressed themselves and went in the direction from which the music was coming.

After playing for some time, Xianiyazi suddenly remembered his cows. He stood up quickly, knocking his cap off on a branch and revealing his golden hair and handsome face. As soon as Nuerbaowa saw him, she fell in love with him.

The next day Xianiyazi picked a bunch of flowers from the old woman's garden and tied a message to it. Then he went off as usual to pasture the cows. At midday he again saw the girls bathing and quickly threw the bunch of flowers into the river, letting it drift down with the current. As luck would have it, it was Nuerbaowa who found the flowers. When she read the note, she found that it was a love letter from Xianiyazi. "My heart is burning with love," she thought. "I never thought that he had the same feelings. Now our hearts are one. How beautiful it would be if we could be united!" But she hid her secret from all the other girls.

One day, when the girls were bathing, Nuerbaowa at last confided her secret to her closest friend and asked her to go off with the others, while she secretly went in search of Xianiyazi. When the two lovers came face to face, they talked and talked, expressing their most heartfelt feelings to each other. From then on Xianiyazi and Nuerbaowa spent many happy hours together.

Time passed quickly and one day, as they were walking along together, Xianiyazi said, "Wouldn't it be wonderful if we could spend our lives together!" Hearing this, Nuerbaowa was delighted, but replied coyly, "Yes. But you must find some matchmakers to discuss it with my parents first."

That evening, after supper, Xianiyazi sat at the old woman's side. He hemmed and hawed and then finally blurted out, "Ma! There is something I would like to ask you. . . ."

"What is it, my child?" replied the old woman. "If you can't tell your Ma, who can you tell?"

"Ma, I really like Nuerbaowa. Could you be a matchmaker for me and go and discuss it with her parents?"

"Aiyaya!" replied the old woman. "I'm only a poor old widow, my child. And you are just an orphan in my care. Those people are the renowned Bayi family, how could they even consider giving their daughter in marriage to the likes of us? As the saying goes: 'Nobility marries nobility, commoner marries commoner and the poor marry the poor.' If paupers like us were to go to the Bayi household to discuss marriage, what would people think? Now forget all this nonsense!"

Not put off by what the old woman said, Xianiyazi pleaded with her three times, saying, "Please, mother. Try at least once!"

The old woman was kind-hearted and finally, so as not to upset him, she agreed to Xianiyazi's request. The next day she got up at dawn and, carrying her water-bucket and broom, she went to the gate of the Bayi mansion. After sweeping the ground clean, she stood at the gate and sang:

> *A matchmaker am I, come to propose a match.*
> *Xianiyazi sends me, please will you reply?*

Inside the compound, Nuerbaowa's parents were just waking up and hearing somebody singing outside, they got up to see who it was. But when they looked out, they found nobody there. Seeing the ground in front of the gate swept clean, they at once realized that a matchmaker must have been there. They looked at each other and waited for her return.

That evening the old woman arranged with some of her neighbours to accompany her to the Bayi mansion. After discussing household matters for a while, she eventually came to talk of Xianiyazi. The Bayis then asked who this Xianiyazi was, what official posts his parents held and how much property they possessed. The old woman replied, "Xianiyazi is an orphan, presently living under my roof."

Hearing this, Mr. Bayi was furious and shouted, "I am Bayi, famous throughout this town! Do you really expect me to let my daughter marry a pauper? This is really too preposterous. Get out of here at once and never dare set foot in here again! If you do, I'll have your legs broken!"

Then the old woman and her neighbours were thrown out. Returning home, the old woman said to Xianiyazi, "Well, I did as you asked. But it is no good. As the saying goes, 'Do not push things beyond their limit.' Did you really expect them to let their daughter marry the likes of us? Best put the whole business out of your head. Otherwise you will suffer for nothing. Now let your Ma find a pretty, suitable young girl for you."

"Don't worry, Ma," said Xianiyazi. "There is nothing in the world which is impossible." He made up his mind to go and discuss the matter with Nuerbaowa herself and try to find a solution.

But from that day on, he could not find his love. After Bayi had thrown the old woman out, he had shut Nuerbaowa up in the family compound and would not permit her to go out. In despair, Nuerbaowa at last asked her closest sister to give Xianiyazi a letter which said:

I have been shut up at home and have no free-dom at all. I really want to discuss things with you.

Tonight, follow the river to our back garden. There you will find an opening in the wall. Climb in and hide in the bushes. I will come out to look for you at midnight.

That night, Xianiyazi did as he had been told and waited for Nuerbaowa in the bushes. Meanwhile, Nuerbaowa lay wide awake in her bed and when midnight came, she crept into the garden. The two of them met and talked and talked. Eventually they decided to run away together on a set day.

At last the day they had been longing for arrived. Nuerbaowa asked the groom to saddle two fleet-footed horses and wait outside the back of the garden. Then deep in the night, she wrapped up a few clothes in a blanket and tiptoed out. When her father came in with his lantern to take a look at her, he saw the bedclothes piled high and, assuming Nuerbaowa fast asleep, he turned round and went out.

Meanwhile, the old groom had prepared two horses and was waiting outside the garden as arranged. Nuerbaowa and Xianiyazi thanked him for his help and then rode off to the old woman's house. When she learned that the two of them wanted to run away the old woman was most miserable and sang:

> *Out there are high mountain peaks;*
> *How will you get across them?*
> *In the lonely desert there are wolves and jackals;*

How will you survive?
Vast forests flank great rivers;
How will you get through?
There are bandits and robbers on the way;
What, then, will you do?

As she sang, the old woman wept, trying desperately to persuade Xianiyazi not to leave. But Xianiyazi sang in reply:

I'm not afraid of mountain peaks;
My noble steed will help me cross.
Jackals and wolves cannot scare me;
A bullet from my rifle will take care of them!
What do I care about vast forests?
I have fire to help me burn a way.
Bandits and robbers cannot scare me;
For I have faith in my destiny!

Despite her anguish, the old woman knew that if they did not run away, they would all be in for serious trouble. So she said to the young couple, "Well, my children, may God protect you!"

Then, bidding farewell to the old woman, they mounted their horses and set off. After many days they reached the foot of a high, steep mountain. Without hesitation, their horses crossed the lofty peaks and soon they had reached the far side. Just then, they saw five wolves leaping towards them, their mouths wide open. Xianiyazi raised his gun and fired three shots, at which the wolves

25

ran away in terror. When they reached a great river and found their way blocked by a vast forest, they quickly lit a fire and blazed a path all the way through to the great road. On they went and before long they found themselves confronted by seven robbers, who shouted fiercely at Xianiyazi, "Your money or your life!"

Xianiyazi replied, "What? I don't understand what you mean."

"If you want to save your own skin," said one of the robbers, "you'd best leave the horses and the girl with us, and get out of here. If you want to keep your possessions, then you mustn't expect to get home alive!"

"Take the horses if you want," Xianiyazi replied firmly. "But this woman is my wife and I couldn't possibly desert her."

Hearing this, the robbers rushed up and knocked Xianiyazi to the ground. Then they ordered Nuerbaowa to go with them to cook their food. Nuerbaowa, thinking that Xianiyazi had been killed, was heartbroken. As she cooked food for the robbers, she planned her revenge. After a while she remembered that she had hidden some poison in her clothing, just in case of emergencies. She sprinkled the poison in the food and then gave it to the robbers. The robbers cheerfully started their meal. Before long their eyes started rolling and, one after another, they collapsed dead on the ground.

As luck would have it, Xianiyazi had only been knocked unconscious and Nuerbaowa quickly revived him with

cold water. Then she dressed his wounds and helped him onto his horse.

After travelling for several days they at last reached Xianiyazi's home village. There they settled down to begin their joyful new life together.

Translated by Stephen Hallett
Illustrated by Sha Gengshi

Xiawudong, the Fisherman's Son

(Uygur Nationality)

There was once an old fisherman who had an only son, named Xiawudong. The old man's wife had long since passed away, and he and his son lived in poverty, depending entirely upon their daily catch. One day, they were sitting by the river casting their nets when all of a sudden they caught a great carp. They were delighted at their luck, but though they strained with all their might, they were unable to pull the huge fish out of the water. It seemed that the only way would be to chop the fish up and bring it to land piece by piece. So the old man told his son to go home and fetch an axe.

Xiawudong searched high and low, but he could not find the axe anywhere. Returning to the riverside empty-handed he said, "I've looked everywhere, but there's no sign of that axe. I don't know where you put it!"

"Stupid child!" replied the old man angrily. "You can't even find an axe! Come here and hold the net. And whatever you do, don't let that carp go!"

At that, the old man handed the lines to Xiawudong

and went off to look for the axe himself. The minute his father left, the carp started pleading with Xiawudong, saying, "Please save me, my child! I have sons and daughters to look after. If you save me, we will be eternally grateful to you. If you are ever in trouble, I will help you."

"Yes," thought Xiawudong, "this fish's life is also precious. Why shouldn't I let it go? But what about my father?"

Xiawudong thought for a long time, but could not decide what he should do.

"What's the matter?" asked the carp.

Xiawudong replied, "I really want to let you go, but my father has such a temper that I dare not. Yet if I don't release you, I'll feel terribly guilty. I just can't make up my mind."

"This is what you can do," said the carp. "Wait until your father returns and then I'll wriggle and jump about in the net as wildly as I can. You pretend that you are unable to hold on any longer and let me go. If your father wants to beat you, just jump into the river and I'll come and save you."

The old man came running back with his axe. Immediately the carp began to leap around in the net, while Xiawudong strained at the lines shouting, "Help! Come quickly. I can't hold on. . . ." At that he released the net and the carp disappeared into the depths of the river.

Now the old man had been a fisherman all his life, but never before had he managed to catch such a huge carp. Seeing his son release this fish, he was livid with fury and rushed at him with his axe. Xiawudong was terrified and leapt into the river. Knowing that Xiawudong was in trouble, the carp swam up and swallowed him in one gulp. Then she swam a great distance until they reached the bottom of a deep pool. Xiawudong spent seven days inside the carp's belly. On the seventh day he pleaded with her, saying, "I want to go back to dry land, to be amongst my own kind once again."

The carp agreed and said, "Since you saved my life, I promised in the future to help you in every way I can.

If you are ever in trouble, all you need to do is come to this pool and I'll come and save you."

Then the great carp thrust her head out of the water and spat Xiawudong out onto the bank of the river. Looking round him, he saw that he was in a vast desert. "I had best follow the river," he thought. "That way I'm bound to reach a settlement sooner or later."

He walked through the desert for a whole day and finally reached a great gorge. A cool, clear stream bubbled out of the rocks, which were surrounded by lush trees and grass. Many different kinds of flowers and grass grew here and the birds sang sweetly in the trees. Admiring this lovely scene, Xiawudong thought to himself, "Why don't I stop and rest here for a while?" So saying he lay down in the grass to take a nap. But just as he was dozing off, there suddenly came a loud "chichaka chichaka" and looking up, Xiawudong saw two young vultures sitting at the top of a cliff, staring in terror as a great black python came out of a hole and made its way up the cliff towards them. Xiawudong rolled over, stood up and rounding the bottom of the cliff, he picked up a large stone and brought it down on the python's head. The python lay on the ground dead.

Seeing that Xiawudong had killed the python the vulture chicks were delighted and said, "Whoever it was that killed that snake, we really ought to repay him for his kindness."

Hearing this, Xiawudong made his way up the rocks

until he reached the nest. The chicks stroked his face with their wings and said gratefully, "If it hadn't been for you, we would certainly have been eaten up by that python. We must tell our parents and ask them to repay you. They should be back any moment. If you wait here they are bound to think you mean harm and may well attack you, so you'd best come and hide under our wings."

So saying, they quickly covered Xiawudong with their wings. Before long, the sky suddenly grew dark, thick clouds appeared and a fierce wind blew. Bushes were flattened against the ground and yellow sand filled the air, obscuring the sun. Then, two huge vultures flew down out of the thick clouds, circled three times above the cliff and landed by the nest. They carried a large hedgehog, which they placed in front of the two chicks. Normally, the chicks would have been upon the prey at once, but this time they just stared blankly at their parents without moving. The two big birds thought this behaviour most peculiar and asked, "What's the matter with the two of you today?"

The chicks replied in chorus, "If you come across a kind-hearted person, how should you treat him? With kindness or contempt?"

"With kindness, of course," their parents replied.

"Today," said the chicks, "someone came and killed that python and saved our lives."

Then one of the chicks pointed at the python lying dead on the ground. Realizing what had happened, the big birds at once asked, "Where is this person now?"

At this, the other chick raised its wing, revealing Xiawudong and said, "This is the person who saved us!"

The two big vultures looked at the chicks and then nodded their heads at Xiawudong in a kind of greeting. "For years," they said, "we have been unable to raise our chicks, for year after year they have always been eaten by that snake. Now you have rid us of this terror." Then, brushing his face with their wings they went on, "We must repay you for your kindness. If there is anything you want, we will certainly help you as best we can."

"Thank you," replied Xiawudong, "but at present I do not want anything."

Then one of the vultures plucked a feather from under its wing and gave it to Xiawudong, saying, "If in the future you have any trouble, all you need to do is burn this feather and I'll at once come to your aid."

Xiawudong took the feather and started climbing back down the cliff. But the vulture shouted, "Climb on my back!" Flying like an arrow, he put Xiawudong down on a flat piece of ground. Xiawudong went on his way and after another day's travel came to the foot of a mountain. Here he saw a hunter taking aim at a fox, which was running around in panic with nowhere to hide. Xiawudong thought to himself, "That fox may have children too. What will become of them if he is killed?"

Just as the hunter was about to shoot, Xiawudong ran over and stood in the way, shouting, "Spare him, uncle!

If you kill him, what will become of his children?"

At this, the hunter lowered his gun and walked off. The fox was very grateful to Xiawudong and said, "That really was very good of you, my child! How can I ever forget such kindness? If you have any request, please tell me and I will do all I can to help you."

But Xiawudong replied, "At the moment, I have no request at all."

"Well," said the fox, "if you are ever in trouble all you need to do is come to the foot of this mountain and light a fire. No matter how far away I am, I promise I'll run here at once to help you." And with that, the fox scampered off.

Xiawudong went on his way again, and after another day reached a large town. Looking about him at the hustle and bustle, he suddenly noticed a crowd of people coming along the street. Curious to find out what was going on, he asked an old man to tell him where all these people were going. The old man replied, "Don't you know, my child? We're all off to the execution ground."

"The execution ground!" Xiawudong said. "What is that?"

"It's the place where people are killed," replied the old man. "Today a young man is to be beheaded there, so we're off to watch the fun!"

"Why is he going to be beheaded?" Xiawudong persisted in asking. "What crime has he committed?"

"You may well ask, my child!" the old man replied,

"That young fellow is neither a murderer nor a thief. In fact, he hasn't committed any crime at all! He just failed to meet the marriage requirements."

"Marriage requirements! What are they?"

It turned out that in this city there lived a king who had a beautiful daughter. The princess possessed a magic mirror through which she could see all of heaven and earth. Many young men came to ask her hand in marriage, but not one had so far met with success. For the princess had made a condition: whoever wished to marry her had first to find a safe place in which to hide for three days. On the third day, the princess would carry her mirror to the top of the gate tower. If she failed to find him, she would accept him in marriage. But if she spotted him in her mirror, he would be sought out and executed. Many a suitor had met his end in this way and now this young man was about to be killed for the same reason.

When Xiawudong heard this he thought to himself, "This kind of marriage requirement is really too cruel! Unless someone puts an end to it soon, who knows how many young men will die?"

So he went to the gate of the king's palace and said to the guard, "I believe that your noble princess wishes to get married, so I have come from afar to ask for her hand. I beg of you to convey my request to the princess and inform me of the requirements."

The guard reported to the princess, who replied, "All right then! You tell that young man that from this moment on he must find a place to hide. On the third day I'll hold up my mirror and look for him."

The guard told this to Xiawudong, who thought to himself, "I had best go and ask the help of the giant carp." He walked along the bank of the river for three days without stopping, until at last he reached the deep pool. He leapt into the water and at once the giant carp swam up and asked, "What can I do for you, my friend?"

"Please hide me somewhere safe," replied Xiawudong. "If you can prevent my being discovered, I'll be able to save the lives of many young people. But if I am found, I will be killed."

"Of course I will help you," said the carp. She opened her mouth wide, swallowed Xiawudong and then swam to the depths of the pool. Then she ordered all the small fish to swim around stirring up the mud with their tails and making the water dark and murky. Before long, the clear pool had become so muddy that the sun's rays could no longer penetrate its depths.

At the appointed time, the princess mounted the gate tower and held her magic mirror aloft. First she searched the mountains, the grasslands and the deserts. Then she searched amongst the clouds. But nowhere could she find Xiawudong. Finally she decided to peer into the rivers and lakes and at once she saw clearly where he was hidden. Near the surface of the river, she saw many small fish, swimming around stirring up the mud. Further down, in a deep pool, lay a large carp, in whose belly Xiawudong lay fast asleep.

The princess announced her discovery and then sent an order to her courtiers, saying, "Follow the river for three days and in a deep pool you will find a large carp. The young fellow is asleep in the carp's belly. You may have difficulty finding him, as the water there is very murky. So you will first have to drive the small fish away and then wait until the water clears. Go at once, and make sure you bring him back with you!"

The courtiers took many soldiers with them and after three days reached the upper reaches of the river. First, as instructed, they drove away the small fish. Once the water had cleared they went to the pool and saw the carp lying in its depths. At once the soldiers were ordered to cast their nets. As they did this they shouted, "Young man! Our princess has already found you. Come out at once to honour your vow!"

Roused from his sleep, Xiawudong thought, "Well, I can't go back on my word." Then he said to the carp, "I had better go. Please take me back to the surface."

The carp thrust her head out of the water and spat him out onto the bank. Then the courtiers and soldiers took Xiawudong to the princess. Now many a young man had died as a result of the princess' requirements, but most had chosen to hide in caves or in the desert where they were easily discovered. Up till now, none had tried to hide inside the belly of a carp and everyone considered this most exceptional. So just as the princess was about to issue the order to have Xiawudong executed, the king intervened, saying, "Wait a moment, my daughter. Do not have him killed yet. If you respect your father's wishes, spare him and let him go and hide once again."

So as not to hurt her father's feelings the princess said to Xiawudong, "I'll let you off this once. Now go and find somewhere else to hide!"

"Where can I hide this time?" thought Xiawudong. Then he remembered what the big vulture had said to him and went off at once to the desert to burn the feather. Before long thick clouds gathered, a great wind arose and the sky turned black. Then the big vulture descended from the clouds, circled three times and landed at Xiawudong's feet.

"My friend," he said, "what trouble brings you here?"

Xiawudong told him all that had happened and then said, "My friend, I desperately need somewhere safe to hide. Please help me."

The vulture told Xiawudong to climb on his back, but warned him, "Whatever you do, don't lock down, or you may become dizzy and fall."

Xiawudong did as he was told and at once they flew up into the clouds. After three days the princess mounted the gate tower and held her mirror aloft. She searched in all directions, peered into the rivers and the lakes, but could find no trace of him. At last, she decided to look into the sky and there, sure enough, she spotted Xiawudong riding on the back of a big vulture, high up in the clouds.

"I've found him!" she said triumphantly to her courtiers, "but this time it will be more difficult to catch him. He's up in the sky riding on a vulture and no amount of shooting or shouting will bring him down. So here is my plan: I've often noticed that after a long flight, the vulture likes to come down to drink at a certain pool. Go to that pool and hide yourselves in the reeds next to it. When the vulture descends that young fellow will probably get off its back. Rush out, drive the bird away and grab the young man."

The courtiers took many soldiers with them and went to find the pool. When they got there they hid in the reeds as instructed. After flying for three days and three nights the great vulture began to feel very thirsty, so he flew down to the pool to have a drink. Just as Xiawudong was dismounting, the soldiers and courtiers rushed out of the reeds shouting at the top of their voices. The vulture at once took fright and flew away, and Xiawudong was once again dragged back to see the princess.

This time everyone was even more astonished at what Xiawudong had done. Just as the princess was about to issue the order for his execution, the queen intervened, saying, "My daughter! If you respect your mother's wishes, please spare him just this once. As the saying goes, 'Third time lucky'. You had better let him hide once again."

Not wanting to hurt her mother's feelings, the princess agreed and said to Xiawudong, "All right then! For my mother's sake, I'll let you off once more. But remember, this is your last chance. The conditions are the same as before. If I find you, that will be the end of you. If not, I'll agree to marry you."

Xiawudong knew well that if he was discovered this time there would be nobody to save him. What was he to do? After thinking for a while he at last remembered the promise which the fox had made and decided to go and seek his help. After walking for a day he eventually reached the foot of the mountain and gathering some dry leaves, he quickly lit a fire. Before long the fox, seeing the smoke,

41

came running along and asked Xiawudong, "What is the matter, my friend? Is there anything I can do to help you?"

Xiawudong told the fox all that had happened and pleaded with him to save his life. Quite unperturbed, the fox said, "That's easy! Why didn't you come to me the first time? Just wait here a moment!"

Then the fox started burrowing into the ground and after a while, disappeared from sight, while Xiawudong waited anxiously for him to return. He waited and waited, but the fox did not reappear. One day passed and then another, but still there was no sign of the fox. Xiawudong began to think that his end was drawing near, for the princess would soon be mounting the gate tower. There seemed no way out.

Just then, the fox popped out of the hole and said, "Ah, my friend! Climb down into this hole at once. I have dug a tunnel which reaches as far as the gate tower. The roof of the tunnel is very close to the surface of the ground and there's even a little hole to let the sunlight in. Go to the end of the tunnel and wait there. The princess will never be able to find you and she'll just have to agree to marry you. Wait until she comes down from the gate tower and just as she passes the little spyhole, break through the ground with your head and climb out of the tunnel. Then run over to her, embrace her and that will be that! Now hurry, my friend. I wish you luck!"

With that, the fox ran back into the hills. As Xia-wudong hurriedly made his way along the tunnel,

the princess was already mounting the gate tower. She held her mirror aloft and began to search the mountains and valleys, the deserts and grasslands. Then she looked into the rivers and lakes and scanned the heavens — but she could find no trace of Xiawudong. All this time he was getting closer and closer to the gate tower. It never occurred to the princess to search the ground directly beneath her. Quite dispirited she finally gave up and descended from the gate tower, saying to herself, "Young man, wherever you are, come to me. I am ready to honour my vow and become your wife."

Hearing this, Xiawudong broke through the ground with his head, leapt out and grabbed the princess' arm. The king agreed to let Xiawudong marry his daughter. He assembled his entire court — forty-one officials in all — and held a splendid wedding feast in honour of Xiawudong. But just as the wedding ceremony was about to begin, Xiawudong, in the presence of the entire royal family and all the nobility of the kingdom, said very politely, "Thank you, Your Highness, but I am just a fisherman's son and could not possibly accept such fortune. I did this only to bring an end to these cruel marriage requirements."

And with that, he cast a glance at the princess, bowed to the king and queen and marched out of the palace. Everyone was stunned. The princess' face turned white with fury and without uttering a word she snatched up her magic mirror and smashed it to pieces.

Translated by Stephen Hallett
Illustrated by Sha Gengshi

Hailibu the Hunter

(*Mongolian Nationality*)

There was once a man called Hailibu. He lived by hunting, and everyone called him Hailibu the Hunter. He was always ready to help and whatever he caught he would share with others. In this way he gained the respect of everybody in his village.

One day, as Hailibu was out hunting in the forests, he came across a little white snake coiled up asleep beneath a tree. Not wanting to disturb the little creature, he carefully stepped around it. But just at the moment, a grey crane dived down from the sky, grabbed the little snake in its claws and flew off. In terror, the snake cried out: "Save me, save me!"

Hearing this, Hailibu took up his bow and arrow and shot at the crane, which was already heading rapidly for the mountains. In alarm the crane dropped the snake and flew away. Hailibu went over to the little white snake and said, "Poor little thing! Now go home quickly to your parents."

The little snake nodded its head in gratitude and went

off to hide in the grass. Hailibu picked up his bow and arrow and went on his way.

The next day Hailibu happened to be passing by the same spot and found his path was bloked by many snakes, all clustering round the little white snake. Hailibu thought this very peculiar and was just about to walk around them when he heard the little white snake say, "Kind sir! Maybe you do not recognize me. I am the Dragon King's daughter.

Because you saved my life, my parents have asked me to come here to meet you and invite you back to our palace, as they want to thank you in person. When you go there, you must refuse everything my father offers you. Say that all you want is the jewel inside my father's mouth. Once you have that, you only need to put it in your mouth and you will be able to understand the language of the animals. But you must not tell anyone about this. Otherwise you will be turned into a stone at once!"

Hailibu nodded and then followed the little white snake into a deep valley. The deeper they went the colder it grew, until at last they reached a gate. Then the little white snake said, "I'm afraid my parents cannot invite you into our palace. They are waiting at the gate of the treasury."

Just then the old Dragon King came up to greet Hailibu and very respectfully said, "How can I thank you for saving the life of my dear daughter? This is where I keep all my most valuable treasures. Do let me show you around. If there is anything you would like, just help yourself!"

With that, he opened the door of the treasury and took Hailibu into rooms stacked high with precious stones, gems and pearls. After looking around the first room, the Dragon King led Hailibu into a second and then a third room, until at last they had passed through one hundred and eight rooms altogether. But Hailibu did not so much as glance at a single gem. The old Dragon King was at a loss and asked

Hailibu, "Kind sir! Is there nothing in my treasury which will satisfy you?"

"These treasures are all very fine," replied Hailibu, "but they are nothing more than ornaments and of little use to a hunter such as me. Now if Your Majesty really wants to give me a gift, please give me that jewel which you have in your mouth."

When he heard this, the old Dragon King lowered his head, lost in thought. Then, sadly, he spat out the jewel and handed it to Hailibu.

When Hailibu had taken leave of the Dragon King, the little white snake followed him out, warning him repeatedly not to tell others what he heard, for this would invite disaster.

From this day on Hailibu found hunting much easier. Being able to understand what the birds and beasts were saying, he could easily tell what animal might be lurking on the other side of a hill and then track it down. Several years passed until one day, while he was hunting in the hills as usual, he heard a flock of birds chattering excitedly. "We must get away from here quickly," they said. "Tomorrow there will be a mighty eruption. The mountain will split open and a flood will pour out. Many of our kind will certainly come to grief!"

Hearing this, Hailibu became very worried and instead of carrying on with his hunting, he rushed back home and told his village folk, "We must move away from this place quickly! It is no good staying here. If you don't take my advice, I'm afraid you will soon die."

Everyone was most surprised at this. Some thought Hailibu must be mistaken, others that he must have gone mad. But nobody believed him. In desperation, Hailibu wept and pleaded, "Will you only believe me after you've driven me to my death?"

At this, several elderly people talked to him, "We all know that you have never told a lie, but what possible reason can you give for saying that we should move away from this place?"

"Disaster could befall us at any moment," thought Hailibu. "Why should I let everyone else die just to save myself?" And so, he told them the whole story: how he had acquired the jewel in the first place, how he had used it for hunting and how today, he had heard a flock of birds talking of the impending disaster. He also told them of the little white snake's words of warning, how he would certainly be turned to a stone if he told others what he had heard. As he spoke, Hailibu slowly began to transform, until at last his whole body had become a solid rock.

Seeing this, everyone felt a deep sense of regret and at once moved away, driving their animals ahead of them. By that time, black clouds had appeared and it had started to rain heavily. Then early the following morning, amid rolls of thunder, they heard a deafening roar and in an instant the mountain had split asunder and water flooded the land. Everyone said with great feeling, "If it had not been for Hailibu, we would all have died."

Some time later, they discovered the rock into which Hailibu had been transformed. They called it the Hailibu stone and placed it at the top of a hill. Later generations have never forgotten him and many tributes have been paid to this hero who sacrificed his life for others.

Translated by Stephen Hallett
Illustrated by Ding Cong

The Clever Red Fox

(Mongolian Nationality)

Long, long ago there was a poor boy named Baololedai. He was quite alone in the world, and dwelt in a little hut where he lived on mice and small birds. One day, some hunters were out shooting in the area. Suddenly, a red fox ran up to him and cried, "Help me, help me! If you save me from those hunters I shall certainly repay you!"

Seeing the fox's plight, Baololedai quickly hid him in a pile of straw. The next moment, the hunters galloped up and shouted: "Hey there! Have you seen a red fox run past?"

"I am just a poor boy," Baloledai replied, "and I have nothing in the world but this hut. There is nowhere here for a fox to hide. But I think I saw one running past here a while ago."

The hunters quickly rode off in the direction he had pointed and the fox was spared. The following day the fox came to Baloledai's hut again and said, "Since you showed such kindness in saving my life, please allow me to arrange for the daughter of Lord Hurmusut to become your wife."

Baololedai replied, "How could a pauper like me ever hope to marry Lord Hurmusut's daughter?"

"Don't worry about that," said the fox, "I'll think of a way!"

The next day the red fox went to visit Lord Hurmusut in his heavenly palace and said: "Lord Hurmusut, please will you lend me your scales? There is a wealthy man by the name of Baloledai living on earth and I wish to weigh his gold and silver for him."

Lord Hurmusut was very surprised, as he had never heard of this wealthy man before. He very much wanted to become acquainted with him, but kept his thoughts to himself and allowed the fox to borrow his scales.

The red fox took the scales back with him and then scraped them with sand and stones until he had very nearly ruined them completely. A few days later he returned to Lord Hurmusut's palace to return them. On his way he called in at Baololedai's hut and told him to sell all his possessions, which altogether fetched five ounces of silver. Baololedai did not know what the fox was up to, and he began to feel rather worried, grumbling, "You promised to help me, and now you've made me sell everything. I don't own so much as a cooking pot any more!"

"Don't worry, Brother Baololedai," replied the fox. "You just wait and see!"

Taking the five ounces of silver, the red fox went to Lord Hurmusut's palace to return the scales and said, "Lord Hurmusut, I have spent the last seven days weighing all the gold and silver belonging to Baololedai. Now I have come to return your scales. This silver is a small gift for you."

Taking the scales, Lord Hurmusut at once noticed how worn they were and thought to himself: "This Baololedai must indeed have a great deal of wealth."

Reading his thoughts, the red fox said quickly, "Would you allow me to act as go-between for your daughter and Baololedai?"

How could Lord Hurmusut possibly refuse such a happy proposal? Still feeling a little uncertain about this Baololedai, he said, "There's no hurry. Bring Baololedai here, so that I can take a look at him first!"

The fox cheerfully agreed and then ran back to Baololedai to tell him what had been arranged. But on hearing this, Baololedai just shook his head and said, "It's no good. The moment he finds out how poor I really am, he'll be furious. Then I doubt very much whether either of us will be spared!"

"Don't you worry about that," said the fox. "Just come along with me!"

The fox took Baololedai off to see Lord Hurmusut. As they were approaching the palace the fox told Baololedai to go to a nearby pond and cover himself with mud, while he scampered on, all in a fluster and said, "Lord Hurmusut, this is really too terrible! The roads around here are so bad that I'm afraid your prospective son-in-law has fallen into a pond! Send a good horse and suitable clothes at once, so that he can change before he meets you. Otherwise, I am afraid your son-in-law will not be too impressed!"

Hearing this Lord Hurmusut also became flustered and at once sent horses and clothes as the fox had requested. While Baololedai changed his clothes the fox scampered to and fro giving him advice:

"Now when you get to Lord Hurmusut's palace, there are three things you must remember. Firstly, as you are entering the palace, whatever you do, don't look back at your horse. Secondly, once you have entered the palace, make sure you are not caught admiring your own clothes. Thirdly, during the meal, don't make any noise while you eat."

Who would have thought that on reaching Lord Hurmusut's palace, Baololedai forgot every word the fox had said to him? He looked back at the horse, stood mouth agape admiring his clothes and made the most terrible noises while he ate his food. Lord Hurmusut began to grow very suspicious and taking the red fox to one side, he asked, "This Baololedai seems to be no more than a pauper! It looks as if he has never ridden such a fine horse before, had such luxurious clothes or eaten such good food."

But the fox, quick-witted as ever, replied, "Ha-ha! I'm afraid you've got the wrong end of the stick! It is precisely because your horses and clothes are not as fine as those in his home, that he spent such a long time sizing them up. Neither is he accustomed to such poor food as you have to offer!"

Hearing this explanation Lord Hurmusut was most astonished and agreed then and there for Baololedai to marry his daughter.

When Baololedai heard this, he became more flustered than ever and whispered to the fox, "This is really the end! As soon as Lord Hurmusut finds out the truth we'll both be done for."

"Don't worry," said the fox. "Let me first go and make a few arrangements." And with that, he rushed off.

As he was crossing the grasslands, the red fox saw a large herd of camels. He shouted to the camel driver, "Hey there! Who do these camels belong to?"

The camel driver replied, "Who do you think could own so many camels? They all belong to the Fifteen-headed Mangus!"

"Well, here's some advice for you," said the fox. "Lord Hurmusut is on his way. If you tell him that these camels belong to Mangus he will probably have you killed. Tell him that they belong to the wealthy Baololedai and I guarantee that nothing will happen to you."

"Thank you for your advice," said the camel driver. "I'll certainly do that!"

Continuing on his way the fox came across a great herd of horses. He shouted to the horse herder, "Hey there! Who do all these horses belong to?"

"Who do you think could own so many horses?" was the reply. "They belong to the Fifteen-headed Mangus!"

"Let me give you some advice," said the fox. "Lord

Humusut is on his way. If you tell him that these horses belong to Mangus, he will surely have you killed. But tell him that they belong to the wealthy Baololedai and I guarantee that nothing will happen to you."

"Thanks for your advice," replied the herder. "I'll certainly do that."

Continuing on his way, the red fox saw a great herd of cattle. He shouted to the herdsman, "Hey there! Who do all these cattle belong to?"

"Who do you think could own so many cattle?" replied the herdsman. "They all belong to the Fifteen-headed Mangus."

"Let me give you some advice," said the fox. "Lord Hurmusut is on his way. If you tell him that these cattle belong to Mangus he will surely have you killed. Best tell him that they belong to the wealthy Baololedai and I guarantee that nothing will happen to you."

"Thanks for your help," replied the herdsman. "I'll certainly do that!"

Continuing on his way, the red fox came across a great flock of sheep. He gave the shepherd the same advice and then went on until at last he reached Mangus' palace. The fifteen-headed demon asked, "What brings you here, you crafty old fox? No doubt you are hoping to trick me, eh?"

"Quick!" said the fox. "Lord Hurmusut is on his way. You had best hide yourself beneath a rock in your sheep-pen, for if Lord Hurmusut catches sight of you, that will be the end of you!"

Terrified, Mangus quickly hid beneath the rock in his sheep-pen. Meanwhile, the red fox scampered about, telling his servants, "You'd best be careful! If Lord Hurmusut asks who you are, tell him that you work for the wealthy Baololedai. If you tell him that you work for Mangus, he will most probably have you all killed!"

Mangus' servants were so terrified that they all readily agreed.

Meanwhile, Lord Hurmusut decided to go in person to arrange the marriage between Baololedai and his daughter. On his way, he came across great herds of camels, horses, cattle and sheep and was told that they all belonged to the wealthy Baololedai. Finally, he reached Mangus' palace and when he saw how splendid and luxurious it was he was so delighted he could not suppress his admiration:

"Well," said he, "my son-in-law is indeed a very remarkable man!"

"Of course!" replied the fox. "But by all rights, your son-in-law should be even richer than he is at present. The fortune-telling Lama has told me that there is an evil monster living beneath a rock in his sheep-pen. It does all it can to make Baololedai's life a misery. Lord Hurmusut, I beg you to have that monster disposed of as quickly as possible."

When Lord Hurmusut heard this he was furious and at once had the rock in the sheep-pen blown to pieces and that was the end of the Fifteen-headed Mangus.

And so, Baololedai became Lord Hurmusut's son-in-

law and lived happily ever after with his daughter in Mangus' palace.

Translated by Stephen Hallett
Illustrated by He Peizhu

The Magic Bird

(Mongolian Nationality)

It is said that in the hills and forests of the north there once lived a most remarkable talking bird. Kings, ministers and rich men from many countries did their best to capture this bird, sometimes sending men, and sometimes setting out on horseback themselves, but not one succeeded. As for the magic bird, it never so much as stirred. It just sat amongst the dense foliage of a ten-thousand-year-old pine tree twittering sweetly. So many people went to try and catch this bird that a broad path through the hills had been made by their footsteps.

In a country to the east there lived a king by the name of Yirteger. When he came to hear of the magic bird, he thought, "What an astonishing bird this must be. I must lay my hands on it!" So saying, he set out to try to catch it. When he reached the forest, King Yirteger immediately found the ten-thousand-year-old pine and waited beneath its thick canopy. The magic bird did not make any attempt to escape, instead tamely allowing itself to be caught. King Yirteger was delighted at his luck and at once set off for

home. On the way home the magic bird said to him: "You managed to catch me with the greatest of ease, Your Majesty. But as you are carrying me home, you must neither sigh nor keep silent for too long. Otherwise I'll be off in the twinkling of an eye! So as we go our way, we must keep chatting."

"All right," King Yirteger replied. "You think of something to talk about."

"Let me tell Your Majesty a story," said the bird. "There was once a hunter who had a dog. One day he was out hunting in the valley with his dog when he came across an ox-cart piled high with silver and gold. The cart had broken down and the driver was sitting next to it looking very worried. After exchanging greetings, the two men sat down together for a smoke. 'I must go to the next village to fetch a carter,' the driver said. 'Brother hunter, could you and your dog please keep an eye on my cart for me?' 'Of course!' replied the hunter. And so the carter happily walked off over the crest of the hill.

"The hunter waited and waited, but by dusk the driver had still not returned. He thought to himself, 'My poor old mother doesn't see too well and probably hasn't eaten all day.' Then he said to his dog, 'Wait here until the driver returns and make sure that nothing gets pinched. I'm going back to cook some food for my mother.'

"The dog obediently stayed by the cart, keeping an eye on the ox and walking round and round like a night watchman. It was midnight before the driver finally managed to find a carter. He returned to find that the hunter had already left, but the dog was still faithfully guarding the cart. As a reward, he give it some silver to carry back in its mouth.

"The hunter was waiting at his gate for the dog to return. When it saw its master, the dog put the money down on the ground. Seeing this, the hunter was furious and said, 'I left that dog to look after the cart, but instead it goes and steals some silver!' Then he picked up a stick and beat the dog to death."

"Ah!" sighed the king, "How terrible! Imagine killing a good dog so unjustly."

"You sighed!" said the bird, and flew off at once.

Angry at his own carelessness, King Yirteger said, "Why on earth did I forget that I mustn't sigh?" And, returning to the ten-thousand-year-old pine, he captured the magic bird a second time. As they were going along their way, the bird began, "Let me tell you another story. There was once a woman who had a cat. One day the woman went to fetch water from the well, leaving the cat to look after her child, who was lying in its cradle. The cat stayed by the cradle, keeping flies and midges away. Suddenly, a large rat came out from behind the door and looked greedily at the baby's ear. This made the cat very angry and it chased the rat out of the house. Just then, another rat ran out and bit off one of the child's ears. Hearing the child scream with pain, the cat came back in and at once killed the rat, which had run back behind the door. Then it went back to the child and gently licked the blood from its ear.

"When the woman returned she was furious and said,

'I told you to look after my child. But instead you suddenly turn wild and bite off her ear!' And with that, she killed the cat. Then, turning round, she noticed a dead rat lying behind the door with a piece of the child's ear in its mouth. Realizing her mistake, she wept bitterly."

"Ah!" sighed the king, "How sad!" And the magic bird flew off again.

Returning to the ten-thousand-year-old pine tree, King Yirteger captured the magic bird a third time. As they were returning along the rugged mountain track, the bird started telling him another story:

"Once, when the land was in the throes of a terrible drought, a man named Arbai decided to leave his home and flee the famine. The sun was so fierce that his throat soon became parched and he was unable to go any further. He sat down beneath a high cliff awaiting his death. Suddenly, he heard the sound of dripping and saw drops of water coming down from the top of the cliff. Arbai was overjoyed and at once held out his wooden bowl to collect the drops. With great difficulty he managed to fill the bowl, but just as he was about to drink, a crow unexpectedly flew up and upset the bowl with its wing. Furious, Arbai said, 'Heaven has blessed me with these few drops of water, and now that stupid bird has come and spilled it all!' Grabbing a stone, he chased after the crow and killed it.

"Just then, he noticed a little stream gurgling out of a cleft in the rocks nearby. Happily, he drank his fill and then returned to the place he had been resting to fetch his bundle. When he looked up, he saw a huge snake lying asleep at the top of the cliff, venom dripping from its tongue. 'Ah!' said he, 'to think that I was about to drink that venom! It was the crow which saved my life.' He felt so sorry that he began to weep."

"Ah, poor crow," said the king, "Sacrificing itself to save others!"

"You sighed again!" said the magic bird, and off it flew.

"Well," said the king. "I think I have to give up. There is no way to catch a bird like that." And with that he went off on his way.

Translated by Stephen Hallett
Illustrated by He Peizhu

The Shell Girl

(Tibetan Nationality)

There were once three sisters called Golden Girl, Silver Girl and Shell Girl. They were all very intelligent and as lovely as the gesang flower,* which grows in the mountains. Their beauty became famous for miles around. Like bees about a hive, young men would swarm to their home to court them. Golden Girl and Silver Girl were so choosy and scheming, that they considered nobody good enough for them. Shell Girl, however, was different from her two sisters. Though still young, she had a kind, honest heart and wished only to spend her days with a hard-working young man.

Early one morning, Golden Girl went out with her golden bucket to fetch water. She opened the gate and looked out, then leapt back in fright. In front of the gate, blocking her way, lay a dirty old beggar fast asleep. Golden Girl waved her hand and said in disgust, "Move aside. Let Golden Girl through!"

The old beggar opened his eyes a little and replied casually, "What's the hurry, girl?"

---

* A yellow flower, similar to the chrysanthemum.

Golden Girl twitched her lips in contempt and said, "Father wants water to make his wine, mother wants water to make butter and I want water to wash my hair. And *you* ask what's the hurry!"

The old beggar shut his eyes again and said, "I can't get up just now. If you want to fetch water, you'll just have to step over me."

Golden Girl raised her head and said superciliously, "Well! I've disturbed both my father and my mother, I don't see why I shouldn't disturb you too."

And with that, she stepped over him and stormed off in a rage.

The next day it was Silver Girl's turn to fetch water. She took her silver bucket and opened the front door. But when she saw an old beggar lying there she took two steps back in fright and said, "Make way, make way! Let Silver Girl through."

The old beggar glanced at her and said, "What's the hurry, girl?"

Silver Girl was very impatient and glared at him, saying, "Father needs water to make his wine, mother needs water to make her butter and I need water to wash my hair. And *you* ask what's the hurry!"

The old beggar pulled his coat around him, closed his eyes and said, "If you want to fetch water, step over me. I can't get up."

Silver Girl picked up her skirts and said, "Well, I've disturbed my father and my mother. I don't see why I shouldn't disturb you!"

Then, raising her feet high, she stepped over him and went off to fetch water.

On the third day it was Shell Girl's turn to fetch water. She got up early and went off happily with her shell bucket. But when she opened the front door, she started back in surprise, for the same dirty old beggar was lying at the entrance. Shell Girl felt sorry for the old man and gently woke him up, saying, "Please allow me to pass. I must go and fetch water."

But the old beggar just lay there without moving and, barely opening his eyes, said, "I'm not in your way. Just step over me!"

Shell Girl replied, "I haven't disturbed my father or my mother, so how can I disturb you?"

So saying, she lightly stepped around him and rushed off to fetch water, singing all the way. The willow by the river were green with new buds and the water was murmuring gently in its bed. She put down her shell bucket and, squatting by the river, took a mouthful of the cool water, before starting to ladle water into the bucket. Not until it was full did she realized that there was nobody around to help her lift it onto her back. Just as she was beginning to wonder what to do, the old beggar suddenly appeared before her, no longer looking so weak and decrepit as when she had first seen him. Indeed, he seemed suddenly to be full of vigour.

"Shell Girl," said he, "I've come to help you lift your
bucket."

Shell Girl was very pleased and squatted down with

her back to the bucket. But it seemed as if the old beggar was deliberately trying to make things difficult for her, for sometimes he would lift the bucket too high and sometimes too low, and although she tried to stand up several times, she never managed to stand straight. Finally, she had just managed to stand, but the leather straps were too loose and the shell bucket slipped from her back, smashing to pieces on the rocks. Shell Girl felt very upset about the loss of her bucket, fearful that when she returned home her parents would scold her. Burying her head in her hands, she started to sob quietly.

The old beggar, however, was not in the least worried and said, "What is so precious about a bucket? I'll get you another one in no time!"

Shell Girl did not reply, but wept even more bitterly, thinking to herself: How could such a poor fellow get me a new bucket? That wasn't just any sort of bucket. It was made from conch shells. Such buckets are very rare in these parts.

But the old beggar calmly put all the broken pieces together and said, "Look, Shell Girl. What do you think of your bucket now?"

Certain as she was that her bucket could no longer be repaired, Shell Girl couldn't help taking a look. To her astonishment, the bucket was whole again and full to the brim with water. She was delighted and thought to herself: This beggar is no ordinary person. He must be an immortal.

Then, thanking him profusely she said, "Is there anything I can do to repay you for your kindness?"

"I have nowhere to stay tonight," replied the beggar, "so perhaps I could stay the night in your kitchen."

Hearing this, Shell Girl felt rather anxious and said, "I'm afraid my mother will not agree, as she detests beggars. But don't worry, I'll try to persuade her."

"There will not be any need for that," replied the beggar. "If she doesn't agree, just give her what you find inside the bucket."

Shell Girl had no idea what was inside the bucket. But believing the beggar to be a most exceptional person, she pursued the matter no further and set off home.

At home, as she was pouring the water into a copper basin, Shell Girl told her mother of the old beggar's request. Hearing this, her mother knitted her brows and muttered, "How can we let a dirty old beggar stay in our kitchen?"

Just then, there was a clattering sound and something bright and glistening fell from the bucket. Remembering what the old beggar had told her, Shell Girl said, "He asked me to give you whatever I found in the bucket."

Looking up, her mother was delighted to see a gold ring and said, "All right, then. Let him stay a night in the kitchen!"

That evening after supper, the whole family was sitting around chatting. Their father was drinking his buttered tea, while their mother did her weaving. After a while, the conversation turned to the subject of their daughters' marriages.

Golden Girl said, "I should like to marry an Indian prince."

Silver Girl said, "I should like to marry a Tibetan prince."

But, when it came Shell Girl's turn to say whom she wished to marry, she was quite at a loss. Just then, the old beggar walked in and said to their parents, "Let me act as matchmaker for Shell Girl. Such a beautiful and kind girl should really marry Gonzela."

But who was Gonzela? Where did he live? No one in the family had ever heard of such a man. How could this crazy old beggar know anybody respectable? He was most probably hoping to act as matchmaker for one of his beggar friends. So both parents shook their heads decisively, while Golden Girl and Silver Girl whispered to each other, making fun of their sister.

Turning to Shell Girl, the old beggar said, "Gonzela is a good man. Would you be willing to marry him?"

"I don't even know who he is," she replied.

"Just believe me," said the beggar. "I will not deceive you. I promise that Gonzela will make you happy."

Remembering what had happened that morning, she felt that she could trust him and nodded, saying, "I believe you. I am willing to marry Gonzela. But please tell me where he lives and who he is."

"You really are an intelligent girl," said the beggar.

"If you want to find Gonzela, just come with me. If you follow the marks of my stick on the ground, you will eventually reach him."

At that, the old beggar walked out of the house. Shell Girl got up at once to follow him. Her parents shouted furiously after her, "Go, then! But if you regret it, don't you dare come back home!"

All this time, Golden Girl and Silver Girl stood to one side, sneering and making fun of her. Shell Girl went outside but, she could not see the old beggar anywhere. Luckily the moon was shining brightly and she soon managed to find the marks which his stick had left on the ground.

The moon sank in the west and the sun began to rise. After walking for a long time, she came to a wide plain on which many thousands of sheep were grazing. From the distance, the sheep dotted the pastures like little white flowers. Shell Girl saw a shepherd-boy and going up to him, asked, "Have you seen an old beggar go this way?"

"No," replied the shepherd-boy, "but I have seen Gonzela. All these sheep are his."

Thanking the shepherd-boy, Shell Girl went on her way. Next she met a cowherd and asked, "Have you seen an old beggar go this way?"

"No," replied the cowherd, "but I have seen Gonzela. All these cows are his."

She thanked the cowherd and went on her way. After walking for a long time, she came across a man herding horses.

"Have you seen an old beggar go this way?" she asked.

"No," replied the herdsman, "but I have seen Gonzela. All these horses belong to him. If you want to find him, carry on in this direction."

Hearing the replies of the three herdsmen, Shell Girl began to grow rather suspicious. She walked along thinking to herself: What sort of person is this Gonzela? How is it that he owns so many horses? Is the old beggar actually Gonzela himself? Could it be that she was letting herself marry an old beggar? And as she was thinking all this she suddenly raised her head and noticed a golden gleam in the distance. As she came closer, she saw a magnificent palace standing at the edge of the plain.

Seeing a white-haired old man she asked him, "Have you seen an old beggar go this way, kind sir?"

The old man smiled and said, "No beggar has been past here. But I did see Gonzela go by."

Pointing at the palace in the distance, she asked again, "Please tell me what temple that is. Which deity does it honour?"

The old man smiled gently and said, "That is not a temple, it is Gonzela's palace. Go along this road. He is waiting for you."

Thanking the old man, Shell Girl went on her way. Wherever she trod, fresh flowers appeared, as if by magic. There were brilliant colours all around and a sweet fragrance filled the air. A gentle breeze blew, as if to welcome

the arrival of an honoured guest.   As the flowers opened,
they formed a brightly-coloured path, leading all the way
up to the palace.

As she walked up the steps of the palace, the gates
suddenly flew open and Gonzela came out to meet her,
escorted by his attendants. They carried rainbow-coloured

clothes and the finest of jewellery of pearls, coral and turquoise. Gonzela was a handsome young prince, and she fell in love with him at once, agreeing to marry him. Only then did she realize that the old beggar had, in fact, been Gonzela in disguise.

Gonzela sat on his golden bed, while Shell Girl sat on a silver bed and adorned herself in the rainbow clothes and fine jewellery. Then they chose an auspicious day and were married in Gonzela's palace.

Translated by Stephen Hallett
Illustrated by Cai Rong

Zhugu and Kangmei

(Naxi Nationality)

In the rich pastures of the Snowy Mountains there once lived ninety strapping young lads and seventy able young girls. Their sheep were scattered about the hillsides like stars in the sky, their pigs were fat as bears and their oxen strong as elephants. However, all these animals were the property of the rancher Dongben and his wife, and these youngsters were their slaves. Year in and year out they struggled to survive, without so much as a single sheep or a single tent to call their own. Their only possessions were cold, hunger, tears and the love and friendship they got from each other.

Of all the boys, the most able was Zhugu. He knew how to make felt for clothing and till the land, and was skilled at hunting and shooting. When wild animals caught sight of him, they would flee in terror. The most beautiful of all the girls was Kangmei. She knew how to shear sheep, milk cows, weave flax and make clothing. She was also skilled in a variety of other crafts. Now Zhugu and Kangmei were deeply in love with one another. They were inseparable all day long, always helping each other and sharing their few pleasures, so as to wash away the tears of their bitter lives   .

It happened one day that Dongben and his wife grew tired of living in the pastures and decided to move to a more comfortable place at the foot of the mountains.   The herders felt as if a great weight had been lifted from their shoulders and for the first time they had a sense of freedom. Fearing that his absence might encourage the herders to try and escape his control, Dongben craftily sent a messenger to them, asking them to move down as well.   However, once caged birds are set free, they are hard to recapture, and the herders ignored Dongben's message. Dongben resorted to subtler tactics, trying to lure them down by saying: "A tree and its leaves are one; spring water and its foam are one; a rancher and his herders cannot be separated."

He also sent them a white crane, a cuckoo, an osprey, a paradise fly-catcher, a wagtail, a swallow, a deer, a mountain goat and a goldfish, one after the other.   But all his inducements were ignored.   Zhugu and Kangmei and their friends firmly refused, saying, "A tree and its leaves cannot be one forever; water and its foam must part in time.   We herders want our freedom.   We want no more to do with you!"

Dongben feared that the herders would drive their animals away and had nine white stone gates and seven black stone gates built to obstruct them.   He also put up

fences on all sides to prevent the sheep and cattle from escaping.

Zhugu, Kangmei and their companions very much wanted to get away. One day, discovering that they had lost a flock of sheep, Zhugu and the other boys went off to look for it, while Kangmei followed with the girls. After crossing nine spurs and seven valleys, they eventually came to a most peculiar tree, beneath which they found the lost sheep. Now this tree had branches of coral, leaves of jade, flowers of silver and gold and fruit of gems and pearls. Seeing it, the poor herders were overjoyed and sang and danced around the tree. Since they had no ornaments, they decided to pick something from the tree to adorn themselves. One young fellow took up an iron axe and started chopping. But the axe at once became blunt and not a mark was left on the tree. Then Zhugu slaughtered and skinned an ox and made some bellows from its hide. He cut some chestnut branches for firewood and melted three ploughshares into a single blade. He took it to the side of a brook and ground it as sharp as an awn of wheat. Then he took his axe and began hacking at the magic tree.

At the first blow, white splinters flew out, changing at once into silver. This they used to make bracelets for the boys and earrings for the girls. At the second blow, green splinters flew out, changing into green jade, which they used as bangles for the girls. At the third blow yellow splinters flew out. These changed into sparkling pieces of gold, which the girls used as necklaces. The fourth blow brought black splinters, which turned into cat's eyes. The boys strung these around their necks while the girls put them in their hair. At the fifth blow, white splinters flew out. These turned into mussel shells which they polished and then hung around their waists and heads.

Now the boys looked even more handsome and the girls even more lovely. Zhugu and Kangmei sang sweet songs to each other and their hearts were filled with joy.

Having adorned themselves and retrieved their sheep, the young herders decided to run far away to escape Dongben's clutches. Zhugu managed to open up the gates Dongben had built while Kangmei broke down the fences and let the sheep and cattle through. They all poured out, with Kangmei riding ahead on a green horse and Zhugu following behind on a horse with a white forehead. On and on they rode. The autumn rains fell and in no time at all the valleys were filled with flood waters. Just as Kangmei and the girls had crossed a bridge in their path a great wave smashed it to pieces, leaving Zhugu and the boys stranded on the opposite side. The boys went upstream to build a bridge out of stones, but this collapsed almost at once. The girls then tried to build a bridge out of hemp stalks further down the river, but this too fell to pieces as soon as they tried to step on it.

Zhugu then chopped down a pine tree and made a boat from its trunk. He also made a coracle from the hide of a white-legged ram and a third craft out of bamboo and birch. He told the boys to start crossing the river ahead of him. When the boys and girls were reunited they at once set out happily on their way again.

However, Zhugu did not get across in time. His cruel parents had followed him and dragged him back home.

Kangmei waited for him on the other side of the river but there was no sign of her sweetheart. Lonely and sad, she walked up and down the river bank waiting for him.

Her friends had already wandered far away, yet still there was no sign of Zhugu. With no other means of supporting herself, Kangmei at last had to take work as a weaver. She thought of Zhugu as she worked and her tears stained the cloth she was weaving. Seeing her distress, a kind-hearted parrot flew down beside her loom and asked her what the matter was. Kangmei replied:

"Please go and tell Zhugu that in the heavens there are three stars which have not yet returned to their constellations: one of them is me. On the earth there are three patches of grass which the sheep have not yet grazed: I am one of these patches. In this village there are three girls who have not yet been promised to any men: I am one of them. Ask him to come quickly with his golden whip and fine horse and take me home."

The parrot flew to Zhugu's home and passed Kangmei's message to his parents. Hearing it, his parents replied:

"Black clouds can obscure the stars. She is no star without a constellation, she is a solitary black star. Grass withers in winter, she is not fresh grass. In her heart there is nothing but evil. We won't let a son of ours go off to fetch her!"

The parrot returned to Kangmei and told her what Zhugu's parents had said, but by mistake attributed these words to Zhugu himself. Kangmei was deeply upset and thought to herself, "Could Zhugu really have had a change of heart?"

Then she asked the parrot to send another message, saying: "Please tell Zhugu: In the past I said many things to him, but most of all there are three things he mustn't ever forget. Only silver can match gold; only jade can match pearls; and only Zhugu can match Kangmei. If he still remembers this then let him come quickly to fetch me with his fine horse and golden whip."

This time the parrot found Zhugu and told him exactly what Kangmei had said. Thinking of the deep love Kangmei felt for him, Zhugu was only too ready to rush to her side. He felt very anxious about her plight and said to the parrot:

"Please say to Kangmei: A lover's words can never be forgotten. I wanted to go and fetch her in the winter, but my parents hid my coat and shoes and kept close watch on me so there was no way I could get away. I wanted to come in the spring, but it was a time of food shortage and my parents would not give me any food. Still they kept watch on me day and night. I wanted to come in the summer, but it was the time of the rains and my parents hid my hat and raincoat. They watched me all the time and it was impossible for me to escape. I wanted to come in the autumn, but then that accursed rancher came and made me work for him. I had to slave away while he stood there with a bamboo cane watching my every movement. How could I escape from him? I've been waiting so long that

I feel as if my heart will break!"

Hearing this, the parrot gave a sigh and flew off.

Since receiving the first message, Kangmei had been longing for the parrot to return with more news. When the wind blew, she thought it must be Zhugu and would get up to meet him. But there was never anyone there. When she heard the sound of horse's hooves she was sure it must be him, but on opening the door she was disappointed each time. She waited and waited until at last she came to believe that he had, indeed, had a change of heart. She became more and more miserable and wept constantly. Her nimble hands became weak and the shuttle lay unused on the floor.

The god and goddess of broken hearts, Gosh Shegwan and Yozu Adzi, took pity on Kangmei. They left their Paradise and went to see her, saying:

"Kangmei, why don't you come up to Paradise and enjoy yourself? You have suffered so much in this life and despite all your trials, you still have no freedom or happiness to speak of. In Paradise we have soft, fresh pastures, flowers which bloom all year round and sweet springs that never run dry. The tigers let you ride on their backs and white deer pull the ploughs. Pheasants welcome the dawn while muntjacs keep watch at the gates. Cuckoos carry letters and the thrush sings sweetly. There are no flies or mosquitoes. Come quickly! You can teach the other young people how to spin snow-white silk and you will eat the most delicious food."

Kangmei, who was still waiting for Zhugu to come,

stared at the two deities vacantly. Her lips were dry, her limbs weak and her tears had long since run dry. She had waited so long that now, at last, she gave up all hope. So following the advice of the deities, she lay down beneath a tree on Mount Ruoluo and died of a broken heart. When the parrot flew back to look for Kangmei it could find no sign of her anywhere.

Now it happened that the rancher Dongben found that a large brown ox of his was missing. He was most anxious. Seizing his chance, Zhugu offered to go and search for it for him. The rancher agreed and, like a hound released from its leash, Zhugu rushed off. He did not look for the ox, but went straight off to find Kangmei. He searched the mountains and valleys, but could find no trace of her. Heartbroken, he wept and cried out, "Oh Kangmei! Where are you?"

He walked on and on and finally reached Mount Ruoluo, where at last he found her lying dead beneath a tree. He was struck as if by a thunderbolt and in a daze he held onto her, crying, "Dearest Kangmei, I have come too late!"

He wept until his tears had washed the dust from her face and stained her coarse clothes. Then Kangmei's soul spoke to him:

"Zhugu, in the past the two of us were one, until the day we were separated by the river. I sent many messages to you, but there was no reply. You are too cruel!"

Then Zhugu told her how he loved her and explained how his parents had prevented him from escaping and how,

at last, he had given a message to the parrot. Just then, the
parrot flew up and confirmed everything he had said. It

also explained that the first message had been from Zhugu's parents, not from Zhugu himself.

Now that she understood everything, Kangmei hated Dongben and Zhugu's parents more than ever. She sighed sadly and said, "Oh dearest Zhugu! I can no longer be brought back to life. Quickly fetch some wood and leaves and burn my body, so that I can go up to Paradise. I'll leave you my ornaments, which are buried at the crest of this mountain. Farewell, my dearest. From now on we will be parted forever!"

Heartbroken, Zhugu collected Kangmei's belongings and then made a great fire from the leaves and branches. Then holding her in his arms, he cried, "Kangmei, I'm coming with you!" and leapt into the flames.

Zhugu and Kangmei turned into two clouds of smoke and were at last united far above the snowy mountains.

Translated by Stephen Hallett
Illustrated by Zhang Dayu

Hengmei and the Golden Deer

(*Naxi Nationality*)

There was once a poor couple who came to settle in the woods at the edge of Jade Lake. Here they built themselves a log cabin. The husband worked from dawn to dusk tilling the soil and hunting in the hills while his wife laboured, weaving cloth and flax. Despite their poverty, they lived a peaceful, harmonious life, their only complaint being that they had no children. At mealtimes they always set three places and when making clothes, they always made three sets, in the hope that they might have a child.

One dark, overcast evening, the woman was sitting by the fireside weaving, when she dozed off and had a dream. In her dream she found herself at the foot of a cliff overgrown with vines. She noticed a little milk-white stream bubbling out of a crack in the rock, and its sound was as musical as a three-stringed harp. From within the rock came the sound of someone singing and after a while a little boat made of cypress wood drifted out with a golden deer at its stern and a young boy at its prow. The boy was singing as he rowed past the woman and he smiled at her. All of a sudden, a crocodile sprang out of the water and headed straight for the boat. She quickly found a bamboo pole with which to save the boy, but the crocodile turned on her instead, opening its jaws wide. She was so terrified that she broke out in a cold sweat and woke up. When she told her husband of her dream, he said that it must surely be a sign that they would shortly be blessed with a son.

On the fifteenth day of the ninth month, when the moon was at its fullest, she did, indeed, give birth to a son. He was white and chubby, just like the full moon, so they decided to call him Hengmei (which means moon). Hengmei grew like a pine tree facing the sun, with a face like a lotus flower at the edge of Jade Lake and a voice as clear as springwater. His parents loved him dearly. At fifteen, Hengmei was already a bright and courageous lad. He could shoot a mountain vulture with a single arrow and chop down a fir tree in three blows. When the poor boys from a nearby settlement drove their sheep into the hills, Hengmei would often go with them to shoot wolves and drive away leopards. He became great friends with them and they, in turn, would often give him small presents to thank him for his help. Hengmei treated his ten friends with great kindness and often brought them musk and chamois. His parents were delighted when they thought of the kind-hearted and skilful son who would look after them in their old age.

In Beishi Village, below the hills, there lived a wealthy landlord with fifty acres of land and thirty servants.

He and his family ate the very finest food and wore the most expensive clothes. The local people called him Adder, for he was as vicious as a snake. His son, Muhu, was a real numbskull and even more violent than his father. He would ride around, trampling the farmers' crops, killing their pigs and doing as he pleased with their women. Everyone in the area hated this father and son.

Early one morning, Hengmei went hunting. Spotting the tracks of a leopard, he followed them on and on until he was far from home.

That day, as it happened, Muhu was also out with his henchmen hunting wildfowl, but despite shooting many arrows he had failed to kill a single bird and was in a terrible mood. Coming down from the hills, Muhu passed by Hengmei's home, which was hung around with fox-furs, antlers, pheasants and other creatures which Hengmei had shot. This was more than Muhu could bear and in no time he seized everything he could get his hands on, leaving the hut completely bare. In his fury, Hengmei's father took his bow and arrow and shot Muhu in the left eye. Hengmei's mother took a weaving shuttle and hit Muhu on the nose. Screaming in agony, Muhu ordered his henchmen to kill Hengmei's mother and tie his father to the log cabin. Then they lit a fire inside the hut. Immediately the whole place was ablaze. Muhu and his gang swaggered off laughing with satisfaction.

After killing the leopard, Hengmei returned home to find his house in ashes, his father burned to death and his mother's body, bruised and scarred, lying on the ground. Hengmei wept bitterly. Looking up at the sky he asked, "Who could have done this?" But the grey sky gave no reply. Looking down he asked the water, "Who could have been so cruel?" But the lake just glistened tearfully and gave no reply. Hengmei felt the fire of anger burning within him, its flames reaching up towards the snowy mountains above.

Hengmei was now homeless, his only possession in the world being his bow and arrows. During the day he would sing plaintive songs and at night he would stay in a cave and make a fire. But although he managed to keep his body warm, his heart remained cold and he would sit up all night without sleeping a wink. Then, early one morning, he suddenly heard an earth-shaking roar, making the grass outside his cave tremble. Looking out, Hengmei saw a golden deer being pursued by a black tiger. He hurriedly took his bow and shot the tiger. The golden deer looked round and seeing Hengmei, came over and licked his hand in gratitude. Now this deer was a lovely creature; its fur was rich yellow and its horns bright red. Hengmei carried it back to his cave and soon the two of them became quite inseparable. When the weather was cold, they would keep each other warm; if they felt hungry, they would go into the hills to collect wild vegetables.

When the Qing Ming Festival came around, Hengmei took the golden deer with him to sweep the grave of his parents. Thinking of his mother and father, Hengmei felt

more miserable than ever. Pouring out his heart to the golden deer, he said, "Oh, if only you could understand what I say! If only you could know how I have suffered. How am I to escape this pitiful life?"

Nodding its head, the golden deer began to speak: "Tell me, what kind of food would you like to eat, and what kind of clothes would you like to wear?"

Surprised and delighted, Hengmei replied, "I don't want to eat anything special, nor do I want to wear fancy clothes. I just want a sword to get revenge, a hoe to till the soil, an ox to pull the plough, a sack of seeds to sow and a sickle to harvest the crops."

The golden deer nodded three times and went up to the mouth of the cave. Then shaking its antlers and lowing thrice, it beckoned to the clouds. Its voice, piercing as a jade flute, rose up into the sky. The clouds parted and everything that Hengmei had desired floated down to the ground. Hengmei called to the ox, picked up his tools and then returned to the lakeside to rebuilt the hut and till the soil. He invited his ten best friends to come and live with him and everyone was most contented.

When Adder, the rich landlord, heard that the people living by the lake were doing well for themselves, he was furious and asked his son what was going on. Muhu chuckled and said, "Those poor devils by the lake have long since been sent off to meet their maker."

Then Adder called for his steward, Changba, and said, "Go off to the lakeside and see what valuables you can find."

Changba dressed himself up as a beggar and went off to Hengmei's home, where he made such a pitiable spectacle of himself that the kind-hearted Hengmei entertained him like a brother. Hengmei's friends, pointing at the golden deer, consoled him saying, "This deer only has to low three times, and gold and silver will pour down from the skies. So you really have nothing to worry about now!"

Changba was no fool, and while pretending to be delighted, he secretly made a plan. In the middle of the night he seized the golden deer and set off home. He told Adder everything he had heard about the golden deer. Adder was most pleased and hurriedly began burning incense and worshipping the heavens. Then he had a special stall made for the magic deer built of jade, silver and copper. He adorned the golden deer with gold and pearls and fed it on the finest fungus and stewed chicken. Then he dressed himself up in his ceremonial robes and knelt before the deer.

"I am a devout and honest soul," he said. "All I want is a mountain of gold and a sea of silver, a stream of jade and a river of pearls. I only want a thousand servants and a thousand acres of land."

The golden deer pranced around, leaving its droppings all over its stall. Then it kicked out three of Adder's front teeth, making him cry out in pain. Adder left, supported by his bodyguards.

Next, his son Muhu came in and pleaded with the deer. "My father has no manners," he said. "Please forgive him. All I want is ten thousand bushels of rice, ten thousand bushels of grain, ten thousand horses, ten thousand sheep and ten thousand fowl. And only ten beautiful girls. You just have to low three times and I'll promise to call you Grandpa Deer."

Again the golden deer pranced around, leaving its droppings all over the stall. Then it kicked Muhu hard on the nose, making him scream in pain. At this, Muhu ordered the golden deer to be locked up in an earthen cell and fed on poisonous grasses.

When Hengmei discovered that the golden deer had disappeared he was most distressed. He soon realized that his guest must have made off with it during the night and furiously set out in pursuit. He followed the deer-tracks along the road until at last he found himself before the great red gates of Adder's mansion. Hengmei picked up one of the stone lions before the gate and started pounding at the gate until it was opened by none other than Changba himself. Hengmei grabbed him while Changba screamed and shouted in terror, at which a group of bodyguards came rushing along to see what was going on. Hengmei was quite defenceless and decided to try and make a break for it but he was soon captured and dragged inside.

When Muhu saw him, he glared at him viciously and said to Changba, "Lock him up with that deer and then do away with him as quickly as possible!"

In the earthen cell, Hengmei found the golden deer on the brink of death. He heard two of the guards whispering to each other outside the door. They were discussing how it was that Muhu had broken his nose and lost an eye while plundering someone's house. Hengmei felt more furious than ever and thought to himself, "I must get out of here. Otherwise, how can I ever save the golden deer and get my revenge?"

That night, he scraped at the earthen wall with his

hands until at last he had made an opening. Then he picked up the golden deer and ran all the way back to the lakeside. Hengmei and his friends discussed how they might get their revenge on Adder and his son. Eventually they decided to ask the golden deer for ten swords. But the golden deer just lay there, breathing weakly. Hengmei and his friends became more and more worried. Just then, the deer blinked and a tiny creature jumped out of its eye and said, "Adder fed the golden deer on poisonous weeds and she will die after forty-nine days. If you want to save her, you must climb Mount Ruoluo. There you will find a great tree on which grows the herb which alone can restore her to health. Below Mount Ruoluo there is a jade cave in which lies a magic knife guarded by a great golden lion. Use this knife for cutting the life-restoring herb."

The little creature then hopped back into the eye of the deer. On hearing this, Hengmei was overjoyed and at once asked his friends to take care of the farm and look after the golden deer. Then he took up his bow and arrow and set off in search of the life-restoring herb. He travelled for three days and three nights, scaling cliffs and crossing great peaks until he reached a mighty river. This river was so broad that the far bank was invisible, yet there was neither bridge nor boat to be seen. Hengmei was beginning to get quite worried when he saw a great black python, with eyes like lanterns, swimming in pursuit of a brilliant goldfish. Seeing that the goldfish was about to be eaten up Hengmei took up his bow and shot the python. The goldfish then swam over to thank him and offered to ferry him across the river. Hengmei sat astride its back and after three days and three nights they eventually reached the other shore. Then the goldfish handed him one of its scales, saying, "When you return hold this up and call three times and I will come to ferry you back."

Hengmei put the fish scale in a safe place and then trudged on through wind and rain for three days and three nights until he reached a great forest so dense that there seemed to be no way through. Just then a great red ox bounded out, pursued by a swarm of gadflies. The ox was lowing pitifully, but was unable to shake the flies off. Hengmei shot at them with his bow and arrow, but no sooner had he made one swarm disperse than another would appear. After thinking for a while, he lit a fire with dry grass and soon all the gadflies had been burned. The red ox came over to thank Hengmei and offered to carry him through the forest. Hengmei mounted the ox and after three days and three nights they eventually reached the far side of the forest. The red ox then gave him a piece of its horn, saying, "When you return hold this up and call three times and I will come and carry you back."

Hengmei went on his way and after three days and three nights he came to the edge of a glacier. The sunlight reflected off the snow and ice was so bright that he was unable to keep his eyes open. In the evening an icy wind blew up, and his feet and hands were numbed with cold. Just as he was beginning to fear that he would never make it across, he saw a big white dove flying towards him from the east, pursued by a black vulture with claws like knives and a beak like a spear. Seeing that the dove's life was in danger, he shot the vulture with a single arrow, and it fell to the ground. The white dove flew down to thank Hengmei and offered to carry him across the ice. Hengmei mounted its back and after flying for three days and three nights they eventually reached the far side of the glacier. Then the white dove gave Hengmei one of its feathers, saying, "When you return, hold this up and call three times and I will come to fly you back."

Hengmei tucked the feather away and set off once again. After three days and three nights beneath the scorching sun and the icy moon, he at last reached a hamlet surrounded by bubbling streams and fragrant paddy fields. Hengmei was delighted, but soon he noticed an old woman weeping outside her hut. Hengmei went up to her and asked her what was the matter. Pointing north to a cave in the mountains surrounded by black clouds, the old woman said:

"A monster came to our hamlet recently. He ate our sheep and cattle and took our people as his slaves. Ten days ago he made off with my only daughter, Azhi, and I have had no news of her since."

Hengmei at once selected a strong arrow, fitted it to his bow and set off for the mountains. Reaching the cave, he found tall, thick grass at its entrance. Inside there was a large stone building. But there was no sign of the monster.

The only person he found was a beautiful young girl sitting on the steps weeping. When Hengmei told her that he had come to save her, she was overjoyed, but terrified that the monster might return, for a stranger in this place had little chance of survival. The two of them discussed their troubles and worked out a plan. Hengmei prepared a poisoned arrow and then hid himself in the rafters.

When the hideous monster returned, it sniffed the air and said, "Do I smell a stranger here? Do I hear a stranger breathing?"

The girl Azhi laughed and said, "Am I not a stranger? It must be my breathing that you hear."

The monster handed Azhi some raw meat and grain to eat, but Azhi put it aside and said, "I'm not hungry at the moment. Let me first help you to clean your teech."

The monster lay down on his stone bed and opened his terrible mouth wide. Azhi climbed up onto the bed and started cleaning out pieces of raw meat from the monster's teeth with a sharp hoe. Then she fetched a bucket of water, and the monster closed his eyes and gargle. Just at that moment Hengmei released ten poisoned arrows in succession, killing the monster outright.

Hengmei and Azhi returned to the hamlet, where Azhi's mother at once accepted him as her future son-in-law. All the people of the hamlet came to congratulate them. Azhi embroidered a scarf which she gave to Hengmei as a token of their engagement. In return, Hengmei gave her a golden bamboo arrow and promised to return quickly to

take her back to Jade Lake. First, however, he had to go to
Mount Ruoluo to pick the life-restoring herb.

Hengmei left Azhi and her mother and hurried on his
way. After three more days and nights, he finally reached
the foot of Mount Ruoluo. Its cliffs were like quartz and
its peaks like jade. Phoenixes cried from the rock and the
summit was ringed by clouds of many colours. At the
mouth of a white jade cave sat a towering golden lion. Just
as Hengmei was setting his bow, the lion pounced. Hengmei whipped out his sword and slashed at the lion's neck,
severing its head. Entering the cave, he wound his way
until he found the magic knife glistening in the dark as
it hung on the wall. He took the knife and climbed the

mountain. Then he came to a tree so enormous that it blotted out the sky. In the forks of eighteen of its branches grew herbs of many colours, one sniff of which could triple a person's strength. Hengmei tried out his magic knife by cutting at the herbs, at which rays of light shot out. New shoots appeared at once and in no time at all the plants had grown back to their original height. Taking the herbs, Hengmei went happily back to Azhi's home. Then he, Azhi and her mother set off for Jade Lake. With the help of the white dove, the red ox and the goldfish, they managed to reach Hengmei's home only forty-eight days after he set out.

Imagine their shock when they found the waters of Jade Lake thick with mud and the pine forests smouldering. As it turned out, after Hengmei left, Adder had sent his henchmen to capture Hengmei and the golden deer. Finding no sign of Hengmei, they had burned down his cottage and churned up the clear waters of the lake. Meanwhile Hengmei's friends had managed to escape into the forests and were hiding the golden deer in a cave.

The next day, the fourty-ninth day, Hengmei found his friends and gave the golden deer a dose of the life-restoring herb. The deer revived quickly and gave three joyful calls, at which the clouds parted and ten fine horses and ten swords floated down to earth. Then Hengmei rode on the golden deer, followed by his ten companions on their prancing horses. They rode straight to Adder's house, eager to get revenge at last. A furious battle ensued, and Adder's henchmen perished or fled. Adder himself started off for the south on a black horse, but Hengmei shot him from behind, killing him instantly. Changba fled north on a white horse, but again Hengmei shot an arrow which knocked him to the ground. Muhu, driven mad by terror, was also killed. Hengmei then set all Adder's slaves free and divided up his property among the local people. Adder's house and courtyard were burned to the ground.

Hengmei and his companions returned to Jade Lake and rebuilt their home. The men went into the hills to hunt while the women stayed at home weaving. When Hengmei and Azhi got married, each of them decided to act as matchmaker for their friends and so Hengmei's ten companions became five married couples. That day the wine flowed freely, the white cranes danced and music filled the air. Everyone joined in the merrymaking and even Jade Lake opened its great, bright eye to look on in admiration.

Translated by Stephen Hallett
Illustrated by Zhang Dayu

Big Xue and Silver Bell

(Hui Nationality)

Once upon a time there was a mountain far, far away. The mountain was called Tinder Ridge. At foot of the mountain ran a little river, and along the river the land was fertile. Here, flowers blossomed, and the scenery was beautiful.

By this river lived thirty poor families, who had all been brought together by chance when fleeing a disaster. These thirty families shared everything, and stood by each other through thick and thin. They were all united as one, hunting and tilling the fields together for their livelihood.

One of these villagers was a young man called Big Xue. When he was very young he had come to the village with his mother and father. After the death of his parents, Big Xue was cared for by the village folk, who brought him up as if he were their own son.

In the same village lived widow Li, who had an only daughter called Silver Bell. Both mother and daughter were very kind to Big Xue. Big Xue regarded all the village as his own family, treating Widow Li as his mother and Silver Bell his younger sister.

Big Xue was a brave and hard-working boy. By the time he was eighteen he was tall and handsome, strong and tireless, and an expert in all kinds of martial arts. He was especially skilled with a bow and arrow and never missed his target. The wild animals in the mountain stood no chance of escaping when he was around. Big Xue was also very good at planting crops: the crops he planted always grew tall and straight.

One day, when Big Xue was hunting in the mountain, he met a white-haired old man who gave him a magic bow and three golden arrows. From that time on, not even the fiercest wild animal or the most powerful evil mountain spirit could escape Big Xue's magic bow and golden arrows.

For her part, by the time she was fifteen Silver Bell was wise, beautiful, clever and sharp. The flowers and birds she embroidered seemed to be alive, and the townspeople flocked to buy her weaving. She sang beautifully with a voice as clear and melodious as the sound of a silver bell and she was so enchanting that even the little birds and animals would gather round to listen to her.

One day when Silver Bell was in the mountain collecting firewood, she met a kindly old woman who gave her a magic flute. No matter how tired the people were they had only to hear the sound of this flute to forget their exhaustion completely.

Big Xue and Silver Bell spent their time eagerly helping everybody they could. They would share game and firewood amongst the villagers and would help anyone in difficulty. And so they lived happily together with the other village folk.

One year some of the village folk were taken ill with a sickness that made their stomachs swell up. It was very difficult to cure this illness, which soon spread through the whole village. The number of sick people grew and grew. They groaned in pain and their suffering greatly upset Big Xue and Silver Bell. They decided to do all they could to relieve the villagers' suffering.

Now there was a man called Mr Ma who also lived in the village. He had read a little and knew something about medicine. Big Xue and Silver Bell went to see him and ask him what kind of illness this was and how it could be cured. Mr Ma answered:

"This is a stomach illness which cannot easily be treated. However, I've heard that there is one medicine that can cure it. The problem is that this medicine contains two ingredients that are very difficult to obtain. One is a medicinal herb, *malianxian*, and the other is the gall-bladder of the leopard. If you can find these two ingredients the illness can be cured. But you have to find them within three months or the sick will not recover."

When they heard this Big Xue and Silver Bell decided to split up and look for the two ingredients. They asked Mr Ma if he knew where they could find a leopard and *malianxian*. Mr Ma replied thoughtfully:

"Old people say that there is a leopard in the witch's cave at the Ten Thousand Rock Chasm. The leopard comes out of the cave only once a year, usually in the hottest days of summer. Some time ago an evil spirit entered the witch's cave and since then no one has dared to enter it. The mountain on which *malianxian* grows is far, far away from here; it is called Ten Thousand Flowers Mountain. To get there you have to go through the Ten Thousand Birds Cave, and in that cave live all kinds of fierce and strange birds. Few people get through alive."

But the dangers and hardships that Mr Ma recounted did not frightened Big Xue or Silver Bell in the least. On the contrary, what he told them only strengthened their determination to go and find the ingredients for the medicine.

108

Big Xue and Silver Bell each took four companions with them, Big Xue, four boys and Silver Bell, four girls, and they went their separate ways.

Big Xue and his four friends walked day and night towards the Ten Thousand Rock Chasm. They had to cross six high mountains and six deep gorges. When Big Xue's four friends saw the high mountains and the deep, gaping gorges they took fright and, one by one, went home. At last only Big Xue was left. After suffering untold hardships he finally reached the Ten Thousand Rock Chasm. When he reached the entrance of the gorge and looked in, he saw that it was full of all kinds of flowers, plants and trees that he had never seen before. In the trees he saw various kinds of birds. And playing freely amongst the trees were all kinds of little animals. Big Xue paid no attention to the beautiful scenery, but crawled into a mountain cave opposite the chasm and hid there, waiting for the leopard to come out. When he was hungry he killed and ate wild animals and when he was thirsty he drank spring water. He waited there for a long, long time, but did not see the leopard.

One day Big Xue noticed the birds in the trees all flying off with cries of alarm, while the animals all ran away as fast as they could. A great silence reigned. Big Xue, with his sharp hunter's senses, felt that a ferocious beast was emerging. He hid himself in the cave, prepared his bow and arrows and his hunting spear, and kept a careful lookout. After a while, he saw a red light shining from the cave and immediately the whole valley was bathed in red. A ferocious leopard stalked out. As soon as Big Xue saw it, his heart was filled with joy. He took up his magic bow, and shot two arrows in succession at the leopard, blinding him in both eyes. The leopard howled and writhed in agony. Big Xue seized this opportunity and, raising high his hunting spear, rushed forward and slew the leopard. He then skinned it, took out the gall-bladder, and set off home in triumph.

When Silver Bell parted from Big Xue she set out with her four girl companions to find the *malianxian*. They walked and walked. The road seemed endless, but finally they reached the Ten Thousand Birds Cave in front of the Ten Thousand Flowers Mountain. Some of the girls went to have a look inside the cave. It was black and deep and full of strange noises that would make your hair stand on end. Guarding the entrance were several enormous and ferocious birds who glared fiercely at the girls. The four girls were frightened out of their wits, and immediately deserted Silver Bell to return to their own village. Although Silver Bell was terrified as well, she thought of the village folk who were being threatened by death, and immediately she regained her courage. She took up her magic flute and began to play. Hearing the beautiful tune, these strange birds were gradually lulled to sleep. Silver Bell seized her chance and ran through the cave to another mountain valley.

By this time Silver Bell was feeling hungry and began

looking about for something to eat. Suddenly not far off she saw a little straw hut on the hillside, and in front of the hut, a kindly, white-haired old man. Silver Bell greeted him, explained why she had come, and asked him the way to Ten Thousand Flowers Mountain. The old man said nothing in reply, but got up and went into the hut and brought out a bowl of soup and a pancake, which he offered to Silver Bell. When she had finished eating, the old man pointed out the way to the Ten Thousand Flowers Mountain and then both he and his hut disappeared.

The food helped Silver Bell regain her strength and, following the road the old man had pointed out to her, she walked for three days and three nights. Finally she reached the mountain. She glanced around her and found it truly beautiful, covered with many fresh flowers and green plants. Yet she was not in the mood to appreciate these rare plants and flowers. With determination she set out to look for the *malianxian*. She searched for a while, then suddenly spotted a few *malianxian* roots growing on the hillside. She hurried towards them with great joy.

When she got there, however, she saw that the *malianxian* was in fact in a basket carried by a girl wearing a red skirt and two fresh pink flowers in her hair. The girl asked her with a smile why she had come. Silver Bell told her everything. Seeing the magic flute in Silver Bell's hand, she asked her to play for her. Silver Bell had not imagined that her playing would immediately attract a huge crowd. Before long she was surrounded by thirty girls wearing green skirts and blue flowers in their hair, and forty boys wearing blue smocks, with their hair tied in two bunches on top of their heads, each bunch decorated with two red flowers. Soon there arrived another forty girls wearing red smocks, their hair tied in two plaits, each plait decorated with two big pink flowers. They crowded around Silver Bell, begging her to play some more. She thought for a while and then played a piece about the sufferings of the villagers. The mournful sound of the flute brought tears of sympathy to the listeners' eyes, and they quickly filled a basket of *malianxian* and other magic herbs and gave it to Silver Bell. Then the first girl led Silver Bell to the edge of a precipice and told her to look in the direction she was pointing. Silver Bell did so. She saw all the sick people in her village, many of them on the point of death. The sound of weeping filled the whole village. Her country folk were waiting anxiously for her return.

Silver Bell's heart was filled with deep sorrow. How she wished she had wings to fly home and give the medicine to them immediately! Seeing that Silver Bell was deeply troubled, the girl in red asked her to close her eyes. With one puff of air, she carried Silver Bell back to her village in an instant.

So the courageous Big Xue and Silver Bell, fearing no difficulty or hardship, found the leopard's gall-bladder and the medicinal herb within three months. They saved the village folk from death and the village from disaster. Everybody was deeply grateful to them, and with

the support of the whole village, the young couple became husband and wife. A huge wedding ceremony was held for them. From that day forth the people of the village sang happy and beautiful songs again.

Translated by Tania Wickham
Illustrated by Cai Rong

Kandebay the Hero

(Kazak Nationality)

On the banks of the Kalasu River in the Kaladawu Mountains, there once lived a poor man called Kasankafu. He lived by hunting and fishing, while his wife occasionally mended nets or sewed clothes for neighbours. In this way, they managed to live from day to day. One day, Kasankafu's wife found that she was with child, and after nine months she gave birth to a chubby little son. Both parents were delighted and decided to call the child Kandebay. Kandebay grew very quickly. After six days he could smile, after ten days he could walk and run and after only six years he had already grown into a sturdy young fellow. He was immensely strong and nobody could beat him at anything. If a full-grown cow fell into a well, he could pull it out single-handed. Whenever his father went hunting, he would go along to help. He quickly learned how to hunt wild horses and became a skilled marksman, never missing his target. He shot gazelle, antelope, wild horses and *sika*,* until their bodies lay around in piles. With his

---

* *Sika* — a kind of deer.

help, all the poor tent-dwellers on the banks of the Kalasu River lived in peace.

One day, as he was hunting at the foot of the Kaladawu Mountains, he saw a grey-maned wolf beneath a high cliff clawing at the belly of a pregnant mare. Kandebay rushed up and grabbed the wolf by the tail, swung it round and sent the beast flying. The wolf howled for a few minutes, then died with its mouth open. Kandebay skinned it and then went to check on the mare, only to find that it was dying. He quickly cut open its belly and removed the little foal. It was a colt, and Kandebay carefully carried it home. He decided to call the little horse Kerkula and fed it on wild horses' milk.

The foal grew quickly and after only six months was some six feet from head to tail and had a chestnut coat. Kerkula was a fine, fleet-footed animal and would do anything Kandebay wanted — even catch birds while galloping along. Kandebay would speed along on his back, as if on the back of an eagle. He could even catch hold of an onager's tail while on the run. In this way, Kandebay acquired the title "Bator" which means hero and his fame spread far and wide.

One day, when Kandebay was out hunting, he happened to meet a young shepherd-boy, who was crying miserably. Kandebay went up to him and asked, "Why are you crying so?"

The child's head was covered with scars and his clothes were very ragged.

"If your mother had been dragged off, wouldn't you feel miserable?" he replied. "And how would you feel if your father had been taken away from you too?"

"What?" said Kandebay. "Tell me all about it."

His tears flowed like a river as the child sighed deeply and said, "I am the only son of Bator Mairgan and I am six years old. Our enemies came to the village and took away all our animals, not leaving so much as a horse's hoof behind.

"My father sometimes sleeps for days on end, and as he had just come back from a long journey he had been sleeping solidly for six days. The attackers grabbed him easily. My mother wanted to wake him, but those cruel men drove her before them with whips and took her away. So I'm an orphan now, with no clothes and no food. The only thing I could do was to become a shepherd for Dashi Kalabay. I am tired all the time and my lips are parched. I can't go on like this. I want my parents back. . . ."

"If that is all, don't cry," Kandebay said. "I'll go and find your parents for you."

Hearing this, the child was overjoyed and said, "My friend! Why don't you first come and rest at our place for a couple of days before setting out?"

Kandebay agreed to this and went back to the shepherd's home. He hung the wild horse which he had just shot over the fire and started preparing supper. In the evening the other shepherds returned, but there was no sign of the young boy. Everybody waited up for him, but after a long time Kandebay felt so tired that he gradually closed his eyes and fell asleep. Just then, the boy returned, calling to his sheep as he went.

"Why are you so late?" Kandebay asked.

"My stomach aches," replied the child.

The following day the child seemed quite cheerful and went off as usual to graze his sheep. But again, in the evening after everyone else had returned, there was no sign of him. Kandebay decided to go out and look for him and eventually found him lying on the ground. When the child had come to his senses, Kandebay asked him what had happened, but the child would not reply. At this, Kandebay began to get angry and seeing this, the child said, "Yesterday, after the sun had set, six swans appeared and flew above my head, crying:

> *Is there a kind-hearted Kandebay here,*
> *With a horse named Kerkula?*
> *His fame has reached the emperor's palace,*
> *And he rides like a shooting star.*

"I replied:

> *I am the kind-hearted Kandebay,*
> *And my horse is Kerkula.*
> *My fame has reached the emperor's palace,*
> *And I ride like a shooting star.*

"At this, the swans beat me to the ground with their wings and I passed out."

The next day Kandebay dressed himself in the shepherd-boy's clothes and went out to tend his sheep. When the sun was setting and it had begun to grow dark, he saw six swans spiralling down above his head. They asked:

"Is there a kind-hearted Kandebay here,
With a horse named Kerkula?
His fame has reached the emperor's palace,
And he rides like a shooting star."

This time, the real Kandebay replied,

"My fame has reached the emperor's palace,
And I ride like a shooting star."

This infuriated the swans, who began to beat him with
their wings. Kandebay grabbed one of the swan's legs and

the rest flew off. Looking at it carefully, he found it was a golden shoe with some writing on it. After this, he waited several days for the swans to come back, but there was no sign of them. Finally, Kandebay took leave of the shepherds and went home. He prepared a year's supply of food for his parents, dressed himself in armour, took the innards of sixty foals and set out to find the shepherd-boy's parents.

Kerkula flew like an eagle and in no time they had covered a very great distance. Riding day and night, they eventually found themselves before a great mountain whose peak pierced the clouds. At the foot of this mountain, Kerkula suddenly began to speak.

"My friend," he said, "our destination lies but a short way ahead. When you have crossed this mountain, you will be able to see a river, in the middle of which lies an island. This island is the home of the Spirit King. That golden shoe belongs to his daughter and he keeps the shepherd boy's parents locked up in his prison. The door to the prison is firmly locked and the Spirit King keeps the key hidden at the bottom of a great pool where sixty rivers meet. No mortal can reach it. On the hillside there lives a giant who looks after the king's dairy herd. He was captured in battle and has now become the Spirit King's slave. Go and give him some money for a journey, give him your clothes to change into and then set him free. You can then look after his cows. Now take a hair from my tail. Leave all your armour and weapons on my back and let me go. They are of no use to you now, nor am I. When you need me again, just burn the hair from my tail and I'll reappear. Everything else you will find out when you get there."

Kandebay plucked a hair as instructed and let Kerkula go. Then he did all that Kerkula had told him to do: he set the giant free, gave him his clothes and enough money for a journey and then started looking after his cows.

At dusk, he wanted to drive the cows across the river, but they refused to go into the water. Kandebay got angry and picking up each of the cows by hind legs, he tossed it towards the opposite bank. The cows landed on the island in the middle of the river and started lowing loudly. Just then, the Spirit King's youngest daughter noticed what had happened and cried out in alarm, "Hey there! Have you gone mad? Why don't you just shout as you did before, 'Let me through, let me through!' "

When he heard this, Kandebay shouted, "Let me through, let me through!" and lo and behold, the waters of the river parted.

Kandebay continued to tend the cows, until one day the Spirit King called his two sons to him and said, "Today the black mare is ready to foal. This will be her ninth foal. But in the past, as soon as she gave birth, the foal disappeared. Go and keep an eye on her tonight and see what is going on."

Now Kandebay happened to hear of this and that evening, when the princes went to the stables, he crept in too and waited. Before long the princes had both fallen asleep and Kandebay alone kept watch. When it was nearly light, the mare gave birth to a golden-tailed foal. Just then, a black cloud floated in and carried the foal off. Kandebay ran after it and grabbed hold of the foal's golden tail, which came off in his hands. There was no more he could do now, except tuck the tail into his clothing and go to sleep.

The next day, the king called his two sons to him and asked whether they had seen anything the previous night. They replied, "The mare did not foal and nothing happened."

The king felt puzzled. Just then, Kandebay came in and said, "Your Majesty, something terrible has happened!"

"What is it? Tell me quickly," replied the king in surprise.

"I want to tell you that these two are lying! They did not keep guard last night, only I did. By midnight, your two sons were fast asleep. Before dawn, the mare gave birth to a golden-tailed foal. But just then, it seemed as if a black cloud floated in and carried the foal away. I quickly grabbed at it, but only managed to catch its tail. The foal was carried off by an eagle, hidden in the black cloud."

Before he had finished speaking, the king asked, "And what about the tail?"

"Your Majesty," Kandebay replied, "please wait a moment. If I had wanted to use this tail to gain a great fortune, I would never have told you about it. Look, here it is!"

When he took the tail out the whole palace was filled

with light. The two princes felt ashamed and had nothing to say.

"Now," said the king, "the three of you must go off, find that eagle and bring the foal back. If you fail, don't you dare come back here!"

Kandebay crossed the river, burned the hair from Kerkula's tail and at once his horse appeared before him. He mounted, took up his armour and weapons and set off. After a while, the horse came to a halt and said, "Ahead lies a great river of fire. Your destination lies on the far side of this river. Shut your eyes and don't dare open them until I tell you, or else that will be the end of both of us."

Kandebay did as he was told, and after flying on for a while, he felt a hot blast of air and then a scorching heat. After a long time, Kerkula at last said, "You can open your eyes now!"

Kandebay opened his eyes and looked around. He saw that they had reached an island on which were eight golden-tailed foals and one foal without a tail. They were drinking at a golden trough. Kerkula said, "Right at the top of that tall poplar there is the nest of a *sumuluer* bird. Once every six months this bird goes off in search of food and returns after fifteen days. It is away at present, but will be back in six days. If we are to escape from its clutches, we must get away from here as quickly as possible. Now, carry that golden trough in front of you and you will find that the nine foals will all follow after us. As we lead them through the river of fire, we will not be able to go straight back, but will have to take a roundabout route. On the way there are three obstacles: first, we will meet a seven-headed monster; secondly, a great white lion; and finally, a wicked witch. We must overcome all of these before going on — so this will be a real test of your strength. Let's go. We must not delay!"

So Kandebay placed the golden trough before him on his horse's back and off they went, the nine foals following behind. After riding for a while, they saw a mountain before them. Suddenly the mountain began to move towards them. It was none other than the seven-headed monster. Kandebay placed the golden trough on the ground and the foals stayed obediently around it.

Kandebay took up a very heavy wolf-tooth cudgel and, rushing forward on Kerkula's back, headed straight for the monster. Immediately he had lopped off one of its heads and then came back to send a second head rolling on the ground. In this way, Kandebay managed to knock off all its heads, one after another, and the monster lay dead on the ground. Kandebay cut out the monster's eyes and stuffed them in his shoulder-bag. Then they returned to where they had left the foals, picked up the golden trough and went on their way, the foals all following behind.

Kerkula ran so fast that the dust was left far behind and soon they had scaled six high cliffs. Before long, they heard a lion roaring ahead of them. This time, Kandebay left Kerkula with the foals, while he ran on in the direction

from which the sound was coming. After only a few steps he found himself being sucked forward by some strange force and in no time at all he saw the lion's jaws opening up before him. These jaws were as wide as the sky and the force that was pulling him forward was the lion breathing in.

Holding a great golden dagger, Kandebay allowed himself to be sucked forward towards the lion's mouth, cutting the lion clean in two. Then Kandebay pulled out its white teeth and put them into his shoulder-bag.

They went on their way, crossing many high peaks, until the sky suddenly became dark and black clouds covered the earth. Only the brilliance of the foals' golden tails lit their way. Then, from the black clouds, a beautiful and lavishly dressed young girl appeared. Kandebay dismounted and walked straight up to her. The girl looked at him for a long time and then said, "You must be very tired after such a long journey. Why don't you come and rest a while at my cottage?"

This girl was none other than the wicked witch in disguise. Kandebay replied, "Yes, I am rather tired. You go on and I'll follow."

The girl walked on and just as she was about to speak again, Kandebay raised his golden sword and split her from head to foot. In that second, a bright ray of light shot out from the sword and then all went black again. When the clouds had eventually dispersed, he saw that where the girl had stood now lay two halves of an evil old witch. Kandebay cut off her head and stuffed it into his shoulder-bag.

"The area which this witch used to control," Kerkula told him, "could not be crossed by any beast or bird. No one yet knows that the witch is dead, so the *sumuluer* bird is not likely to pass this way. We can rest here for a few days."

After resting there for four days and collecting the witch's treasures, Kandebay once again took up the golden trough and they went on their way. Before long they arrived safely back at the Spirit King's palace.

The Spirit King was delighted when he saw them and welcomed Kandebay with a great banquet. Just as they were celebrating, the king's two sons returned empty-handed. They both looked exhausted and faint and their bodies

were as thin as twigs. The king then invited Kandebay
to the royal chambers and asked him to talk about himself.

"I am no spirit prince," replied Kandebay, "but the
son of common parents. My name is Kandebay and everyone knows me as 'Kandebay with the horse Kerkula'. I
have not come here as an idle traveller, but have a definite
purpose. If you will permit me, I will tell you about it."

"Tell me, my child," said the king.

"Several years ago," said Kandebay, "your troops
plundered our village, driving all our animals away. They
also captured our *bator* while he was off his guard. I have
come to try and have him released. In addition to this,
when I was out in the pastures one day, six swans swooped
down above my head. One of them left a golden shoe in
my hands. I have heard that such a shoe can only be found
in your kingdom, so I would therefore like to return it to
Your Majesty."

Then Kandebay handed over the golden shoe. The
king replied, "What you say is true, my child. It was I who
ordered your animals to be driven away and your *bator* to
be captured. Both Mairgan and his wife are here. Mairgan
is in prison. I once said to him, 'You do as I tell you and
I'll set you free.' But he would not agree to my offer and
said, 'I would never help an enemy!' I fear that he is so
unbending that he will try to get even with me as soon as
I release him."

Then the king continued, "I, too, have heard of your
fame. I wanted to invite you here to tackle that bird which

128

keeps stealing our foals. I looked for you myself, but could not find you. That is why I sent my troops to raid your village and captured your *bator*. I thought that if you really had courage, you would certainly come in search of him. But I waited for two years and you still had not come. So I sent my six daughters to go and look for you. That shoe belongs to my youngest daughter. But I now have another condition for you. There is a seven-headed monster, a great white lion and a wicked witch. If you can dispatch all these creatures for me, I will return your *bator* to you and release all your animals. In addition, I will give you my youngest daughter in marriage."

Kandebay took his shoulder-bag from the back of his horse and pulled out the witch's head, the lion's teeth and the monster's eyes. The king was delighted and at once released Mairgan, his wife and all the other people he had captured. He also returned all the animals and gave Kandebay his sixth daughter in marriage. A grand wedding took place. Kandebay received the greatest of rewards and then returned to his home. When he got back he at once returned all the cattle, sheep and horses to their original owners.

The villagers all came out to welcome Kandebay and then held a great feast. During Kandebay's lifetime, not a single enemy dared to invade the village again.

Translated by Stephen Hallett
Illustrated by Zhu Yanling

The Long-haired Girl

(Dong Nationality)

High on the slopes of Mount Dougao there is a waterfall which looks just like a girl lying on a cliff with her long white hair draped down the mountainside. The people there call this the White Hair Waterfall. And there is a tale about this waterfall.

Long, long ago there was no water near the slopes of Mount Dougao. The people who lived in the area depended on rain both to water their crops and provide them with drinking water. If it did not rain, they had to carry water from a little stream more than two miles away. So water was as precious as oil in these parts.

Now there was a young girl in the village whose beautiful black hair streamed right down to her heels. Everyone called her the Long-haired Girl. The only other person in her family was her sick old mother, who lay in bed all day, unable to move. The two of them depended entirely on their pigs, which the Long-haired Girl raised single-handed. Every day she was busy from dawn to dusk, walking the two miles to fetch water and then climbing the slopes of a nearby mountain to collect pig feed.

One day, she was out collecting roots, her bamboo basket in her hand, when suddenly she found a beautiful green turnip plant, growing from a crack in the rocks above a high precipice. "This will certainly make a delicious meal for the pigs," she thought.

She pulled with both hands and out came a round red turnip, as big as a teacup. From the hole which the turnip had left, a stream of clear water began to flow. The next moment the turnip had flown out of her hands and "pop!" had plugged up the hole.

Feeling rather thirsty, the Long-haired Girl pulled out the turnip again, put her mouth to the hole and took several gulps. The water was cool and sweet, as delicious as pear juice. But no sooner had her mouth left the hole than "pop!" the turnip flew back again.

As she was looking at the turnip, a strong wind suddenly started up, blowing her into a cave. There on a large stone block in the cave sat a man covered from head to foot with yellow hair. He glared at the Long-haired Girl fiercely and said:

"So, you have discovered the secret of my mountain, haven't you? Don't you dare tell anybody else about it. If you do, and other people come up here to steal my water, I will kill you! Remember well what I say. I am the spirit of this mountain."

Then another gust of wind blew the Long-haired Girl to the foot of the mountain. Walking home, the

Long-haired Girl felt very upset and anxious. She dared
tell neither her mother nor anyone else in the village about
her discovery. Day after day she looked at the dry fields
and the villagers, old and young, carrying buckets to the
stream two miles away to fetch water. How she wanted
to tell them about the turnip and the spring she had

found! But when she thought of the fierce, yellow-haired mountain spirit, her words just stuck in her throat.

She felt more and more miserable. She could neither sleep nor eat and gradually became mute, like an idiot. Her eyes were no longer bright and sparkling, but dull and empty. Her once red and rosy face became pale and sallow. Her hair, too, which had once been so black and smooth, looked dry and withered.

Her mother, clasping her hand, said, "My child, what is the matter with you?"

But the Long-haired Girl kept her lips firmly closed and would not utter a word. As days and months passed by, her hair gradually became snow-white and, lacking the will to brush it or tie it up, she would just let it hang loose about her.

"How strange," everyone started saying. "Such a young girl, yet her hair has already turned snow-white."

The Long-haired Girl leaned idly at her gate, watching the passers-by. She would mutter to herself, "On Mount Dougao there is. . . ." But then she would clamp her teeth tightly against her lips with such force that they left a red mark.

One day, as she was leaning at her gate as usual, she saw a white-bearded old man staggering along the road with water he had fetched from the stream two miles away. Suddenly, he stumbled against a stone and fell to the ground. The water poured over the road and the buckets broke, while blood gushed out of a wound in the old man's leg.

The Long-haired Girl ran over and helped him up, then tore off a piece of her clothes and squatted down to dress the old man's wound. Hearing his groans and sighs and seeing the pain in his face, she said to herself: "You are just afraid of death! And because of this, the fields go dry, the crops wither and the villagers sweat and suffer. It is your fear of death that has caused this old man to break his leg. You. . . ."

She could not hold back any longer and suddenly shouted to the old man, "Grandpa, grandpa! On Mount Dougao there is a spring! You only have to pull out the turnip, chop it to pieces, widen the hole in the rocks and the water will rush down the mountain. It's true, it's true! I've seen it with my own eyes!"

Not waiting for the old man to reply, she stood up and lifting up her hair, cried, "Come quickly everybody, there's water on Mount Dougao!"

Then she explained how she had found the spring. She told of everything, except what the mountain spirit had said to her. The villagers had always known the Long-haired Girl to be honest and kind-hearted and they believed what she said. They took knives and chisels and followed her up the hillside until they reached the top of the cliff. The Long-haired Girl pulled out the turnip with both hands, threw it on the rocks and cried, "Chop it into pieces quickly. Oh, do be quick!"

Before long the turnip had been cut up and from the hole in the rocks water began pouring out. But since the hole was no larger than a teacup only a small amount of water could flow out.

"Widen the hole with your chisels," said the Long-haired Girl. "But do be quick!"

Several of the villagers started chiselling, and before long the hole was the size of a large plate, then the size of a bucket and finally as large as a vat. The water bubbled down the mountain and the villagers all laughed with joy.

Just then, a gust of wind blew up and the Long-haired Girl disappeared. The villagers were so pleased with their new spring that they did not at first notice that she was missing. Then somebody asked, "Where is the Long-haired Girl?" "She has probably gone home to tell her mother the good news," replied the others, and everyone came happily down the mountain.

But the Long-haired Girl had not returned home at all. She was brought before the mountain spirit again, who said:

"I told you not to tell others about my water. But you brought all those people up here, cut up the turnip and widened the hole. Now I'm going to kill you!"

Holding her white hair, the Long-haired Girl replied coolly, "I am not afraid to die for others."

The mountain spirit ground his teeth and said, "I won't give you an easy death. I shall make you lie at the top of the cliff, so that the water flows over your

135

body. In that way your suffering will be long and painful!"

But the Long-haired Girl answered coldly, "I am willing to suffer such a death for the sake of others. All I beg of you is to allow me to return home once, to ask someone to take care of my sick mother and my pigs."

The mountain spirit thought for a while and then said, "I will let you go home once. But if you do not return I'll stop up the hole and kill everybody in your village. When you return, lie down beneath the water yourself and don't come and bother me again!"

The Long-haired Girl nodded and a gust of wind carried her down to the foot of the mountain. Thinking of the water bubbling down the mountain, sparkling through the field and reviving the crops, she couldn't help smiling with joy. She went home and, unable to tell her mother the truth, said, "Mother, there is water on Mount Dougao. Our village will not have to worry about water any more."

"Mother," she went on, "the girls in the next village have invited me over for a few days. I'll ask aunty next door to look after you and the pigs while I'm away."

Her mother smiled and said, "Go along, then!"

After everything had been arranged, she went to see her mother again. "Ma, I may be away for at least ten days. You . . ." she said, nearly in tears.

"Go ahead and enjoy yourself," said her mother. "Aunty will take good care of me."

The Long-haired Girl stroked her mother's face and hand, tears rolling down her cheeks. Then she went to the pigsty and patted the little pigs' heads and tails. Once again the tears began to flow.

At the door of their cottage she said, "Ma, I'm off!"

Without waiting for a reply she flung her long white hair over her shoulder and headed towards Mount Dougao. On the way, she passed a large, luxuriant banyan tree. The Long-haired Girl stroked its trunk and said, "Oh, banyan tree! Never again will I come to seek shade beneath your branches."

Suddenly, from behind the banyan tree a tall old man appeared. His hair and beard were green and he was dressed entirely in green. He said, "Where are you going, Long-haired Girl?"

She sighed and lowered her head without replying.

"I already know of your plight," said the old man. "You are a good person and I want to save you. I have carved a stone statue of you — come behind this tree and have a look!"

She went behind the tree, and saw a stone replica of herself, exact in every way, except that it had no hair. She looked at it in amazement.

The old man said, "The mountain spirit wants you to lie on the cliff and let the water flow over you. That would certainly be more than you could bear! Instead, I will carry this stone statue up and put it in your place. At the moment, though, it still has no hair, so I am afraid you will have to suffer while I pull out your hair. In this way, the mountain spirit will not suspect anything."

Not waiting for a reply, the old man set to work pulling out her hair and placed it on the head of the stone statue, where it immediately took root.

The Long-haired Girl's head was now completely bald, but the statue had long, white hair. The old man smiled and said, "Go home, now. There is water in the fields and the villagers need help planting their crops. From now on, your lives will get better and better."

Then the old man hurried off towards Mount Dougao carrying the stone statue. He placed the stone statue on the cliff and let the water cascade over it, so that its long white hair flowed down the cliff-face.

The Long-haired Girl leant against the banyan tree in a daze. Suddenly she felt her head begin to itch. She rubbed it with her hand and realized that her hair was beginning to grow again. It quickly grew down to her heels and when she looked, she saw that it was black, just as it had been before. She waited beneath the tree for a long time, but there was still no sign of the old man in green. Suddenly, a gentle breeze stirred the leaves and she heard a voice saying, "Long-haired Girl," it said, "that mountain spirit has been deceived. Go home now."

The Long-haired Girl looked towards the White Hair Waterfall on Mount Dougao, at the fresh green crops and at the happy villagers working in the fields. Then she looked at the lush, green banyan tree and, with a shake of her long, black hair, she danced merrily home.

Translated by Stephen Hallett
Illustrated by Zeng Youxuan

139

Mola

(Yugur Nationality)

Long, long ago the Yugur people drove their cattle, sheep and camels all the way from far-off Xinjiang Province to the foot of the Qilian Mountains in Gansu Province. On their way they crossed great deserts and swamps, always searching for water and grass as they went. The pastures below the Qilian Mountains were excellent and the herdsman were delighted to see their animals grow fat and strong. At the foot of the mountains, however, there was an ice cave inhabited by a great Snow Demon. This demon made trouble regularly, often bringing great disaster to the grasslands. Whenever people saw clouds of white mist rising from the cave under the mountains, they would know at once that the Snow Demon was in a bad mood. In no time at all there would be a violent snowstorm and thick snow would smother the grasslands for weeks on end. There would be no firewood to burn, the animals would go hungry and the lambs and calves, unable to withstand the bitter cold, would freeze to death.

Time and time again people would burn incense and

kowtow to the Snow Demon, but he was quite unmoved by their pleas. Now, there was a young man called Mola who, on seeing the evil doing of the Snow Demon, felt his heart swell with anger. One day, Mola went to his grandfather and asked, "Grandpa, that Snow Demon is so wicked. Isn't it about time we get rid of him?"

"My child," his grandfather replied, "that demon has such remarkable powers that nobody dares take him on!"

"Is there really nobody in the whole world who can overcome the Snow Demon?" Mola asked.

"Only the Sun God can overcome him, but he lives far away in the Eastern Sea and to get there you must cross high mountains and cover vast distances. Who could possibly go to him to learn his magic and beg his treasures?"

When Mola heard his grandfather's words he beat his chest and said resolutely, "If that Snow Demon can be defeated, I'd quite willing to take the risk of visiting the Sun God!"

Hearing that Mola was setting off in search of the Sun God, the people of the grasslands all came to give him a grand send-off. One old herdsman from the eastern sands gave Mola his precious horse, which could run three thousand miles in one day. An old woman from the western sands gave him her valuable waterproof cloak. A hunter from the southern hills gave him a magic arrow which never missed its target and a shepherdess from the northern hills gave him one of her whips. Amid cheers of encouragement our little hero donned his cloak, slung his bow and arrow over his shoulder and mounted the precious horse. Then, holding his whip aloft, he set out for the east, where the sun rises, as fast as he could ride.

The precious horse carried Mola across expanses of grassland and over great snowy mountains. On and on they sped until suddenly they found themselves confronted by a towering stone cliff obstructing the way. The name of this cliff was the Knife Edge, as it pierced the clouds. On seeing its height the precious horse began sweating all over and trotted back and forth along the foot of the cliff; to cross this mountain seemed an almost impossible task. Just as Mola was beginning to fear that they would never get across, he heard a lark singing just above his head:

Brother Mola, brother Mola,
Of course your horse can pierce the sky.
Why not give your whip a try?

Mola cracked his whip, and there was a great clap of thunder. The whip shot up into the clouds, carrying both horse and rider clear across the Knife Edge. Mola continued riding east and after many thousands of miles, reached the edge of a great forest. This forest was called the Forest of the Black Tiger, for it was inhabited by a black tiger spirit. Seeing a stranger passing through its forest, the Black Tiger gave a mighty roar and leapt out towards Mola. Terrified, the precious horse swung round and started heading back the way they had come, the Black

Tiger following close at his heels.   At that moment Mola again heard the lark singing:

> Brother Mola, brother Mola,
> The Black Tiger can harm no hero.
> Why not try your bow and arrow?

Mola took his bow, fitted the magic arrow and turning round in his saddle, took aim at the Black Tiger. There was a twang as the arrow was released.   The Black Tiger roared and fell dead to the ground.

Mola turned his horse around and once again started galloping east.   After many thousands of miles he at last reached the shores of the Eastern Sea.   Far in the distance he could see the palace of the Sun God glistening brightly in the red glow on the horizon.   But the ocean was so vast and the waves so mighty that the precious horse gave a terrified neigh and would go no further.

Just as Mola was beginning to feel anxious, he suddenly heard the lark singing above his head:

> Brother Mola, brother Mola,
> When a hero meets danger he casts out all fear.
> You have a waterproof cloak you can wear.

Mola put on his cloak, brandished his whip and urged his horse to plunge forward into the waves.   At once he saw the waves retreat as the sea formed a smooth path in front of him.   The precious horse galloped across the surface of the water, straight towards the gate of the Sun God's palace.

The gatekeeper of the palace of the Sun God was one of his female disciples, a young and beautiful girl clad in red and green. Seeing a stranger riding straight towards the palace across the water, she at once cried out, "Hey there! You can't just storm in like this. We'll see what my magic weapon can do to you." So saying, she released a magic eagle which flew over to grab Mola. Mola took his bow and arrow and in no time at all had shot the eagle down, while the precious horse continued to carry him quickly towards the gate. In her alarm, the girl rushed inside the gates, which she slammed shut. Mola dismounted and, thundering with his fists on the great gold and silver gate, started shouting:

> Oh Sun God, Sun God, please let me in!
> The folk of the grasslands are facing great peril,
> I need your weapon to rid them of evil!

He went on banging and shouting until his fists became bruised and his voice became hoarse. For three days and three nights he shouted and banged until at last he managed to rouse the Sun God. The Sun God told the girl at the gate to let Mola in. At last Mola was led before the Sun God's throne. The Sun God wore a red cloak and a golden crown. He waved a gilded fan and his whole body shone with a golden light, so bright that those who saw him found it impossible to keep their eyes open. Stroking his long, red beard he smiled and said, "Well, now, my brave young fellow! I knew of your coming long ago. Now

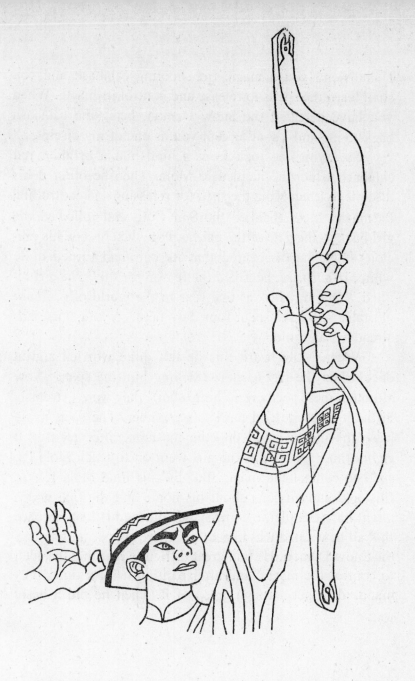

I shall lend you a magic fire-shooting calabash and you shall learn the spells to release and control its magic. When you have defeated the Snow Demon, bring the calabash back to me and I shall accept you as one of my disciples."

So saying, he took from behind him a brilliant red calabash which he handed to Mola. Then he ordered his disciple to teach Mola the spell for releasing and controlling its magic. Mola thanked the Sun God, and followed the girl back to the gate of the palace, but when he saw his precious horse he discovered that its hair had turned quite white. In surprise, he asked the reason for this. The girl replied, "One day here is one year in the world of ordinary mortals. You have spent four days here, so your horse has already grown old."

When Mola heard this he felt quite worried and at once asked the girl to start teaching him the spells. Now although these spells were quite short, they were extremely difficult to recite and hard to remember. The spell to release the magic could only be mastered after reciting it eighty times. After this the girl went on to teach Mola the spell to control the magic. But by this time Mola felt so flustered and anxious about his home and the fate which might have befallen the grasslands during his long absence that all he wanted was to get back there at once and destroy the Snow Demon. He had great difficulty learning the spell to control the magic, and after reciting it forty times only managed to get a rough grasp of it. Then he bid a hasty

146

farewell to the girl, mounted his horse and set off on his homeward journey.

Since his departure, Mola's friends and relations had been waiting daily for him to return and rid them of the Snow Demon. But as the years went by and there was no sign of him, people began to sigh, "Poor Mola! Most probably he will never return."

In the winter of the eighth year Mola finally returned. Tired, footsore and covered all over in dust, he trudged home. It turned out that the horse he had set out on had grown so weak that it died of exhaustion at the side of the road. Not afraid of the high mountains and vast distances, brave young Mola had walked the rest of the way home.

On the day after Mola's return, the Snow Demon started letting out clouds of white mist from his ice cave and there followed the most terrible snowstorm. At once Mola set out to fight the demon. Clasping the magic calabash, he braved the blizzards and made his way to the foot of the Qilian Mountains. The villagers followed far behind, beating drums and banging gongs in encouragement.

Striding to the foot of the mountains Mola quietly recited the spell to release the magic and with all his might threw the magic calabash into the air. In a flash of red light the calabash flew like a fireball straight into the Snow Demon's ice cave. Within seconds the ice cave was filled with fire and the wicked Snow Demon, who had brought centuries of misery to the grasslands, perished inside.

Although the Snow Demon was dead the fire inside the cave continued to burn fiercely. Mola wanted to recite the spell to control the magic and retrieve the calabash, but he found that it had gone clean out of his head. The fire raged for three days and three nights and Mola was afraid that a great fire might break out on the grasslands, bringing disaster to his people. With great resolve he plucked up courage and leapt into the flames to retrieve the magic calabash. He pounced on the calabash, smothering the hole from which the flames were shooting and gradually the fire began to go down. But poor brave Mola was completely consumed by the flames and transformed into a red stone mountain towering above the edge of the grasslands. This mountain is always hot and neither trees nor grass will grow on it. Its heat melts the ice and snow for miles around, increasing the amount of water in the White Poplar River. As a result, the grasslands are more luxuriant than ever, the sheep and cattle grow fat and strong and the Yugur people pass their days in peace and prosperity.

Whenever hunters go hunting in the mountains or herdsmen go out to graze their sheep and cattle they gaze from afar at the towering peak of Red Stone Mountain. Their hearts are filled with gratitude, and they pay their respects to that brave son of the grasslands, Mola, who rid them of the Snow Demon.

Translated by Stephen Hallett
Illustrated by Zhang Shiyan

神　鸟
——中国民间故事选

丁　聪　蔡　荣
沙更士　曾佑瑄　朱延令　插图
张世彦　张大羽　何佩珠

*

外文出版社出版
（中国北京百万庄路24号）
外文印刷厂印刷
中国国际图书贸易总公司
（中国国际书店）发行
北京399信箱
1985年（大32开）第一版
编号：（英）10050—1162
00300
10—E—1769 P